Praise for Lights, C

Kevin Butler is a phenomenal educator who both talks the talk and walks the walk. I have known him for many years, and his dedication to his students and profession is an inspiration to us all. You will learn his powerful strategies for engaging students, building relationships, and creating a classroom where all students can thrive. You would be hard-pressed to find a book that gives more practical, effective strategies that you can implement right away.

—**Kim Bearden**, cofounder, executive director, language arts teacher, the Ron Clark Academy Clark Academy

This book is filled with practical ideas that will hook your students like never before. Not only does Kevin Butler provide ideas for classroom transformations and games, he also provides ideas to help build connections within the classroom and across communities.

—**Deedee Wills**, award-winning educator, international speaker, and curriculum developer at Mrs. Wills Kindergarten

Lights, Cameras, TEACH! is an outstanding book full of inspirational ideas and practical plans for those of us who want to take our classroom instruction to the next level. It takes readers on a cinematic journey into the whimsical world of creating entertaining yet educative spaces for students. Kevin Butler has written a must-read book for anyone considering innovative approaches to teaching, culture, and relationships. Read this and learn from one of the best.

—**Dr. Richard Warren Jr.**, Maryland State Teacher of the Year, educator, and national speaker

Discovering Kevin Butler on social media changed the way I saw the magic of a classroom, so you can only imagine how eager I was to get my hands on *Lights, Cameras, TEACH!* Getting to know Kevin over the last three years has been an honor! Kevin Butler is innovative, dynamic, and continually carries a quixotic mindset. When he shared the dream for his first book, I knew it would have inspirational stories and be filled with action steps educators can implement into their daily practice right away. IT DID NOT DISAPPOINT! I can't wait to grab a few more copies and pass them out to other educators in my life needing a boost!

—**Rae Hughart**, Teach Better Team

Kevin is a passionate educator who brings learning to life in ways that reach all students. *Lights, Cameras, TEACH!* is a must-read for teachers looking for easy and effective ways to bring fun and excitement into their classrooms! I'm excited to bring new ideas, games, and activities into my classroom thanks to Kevin and his book!

—**Greg Smedley-Warren**, Kindergarten teacher, the Kindergarten Smorgasboard

The education system as we know it today is broken, but don't be fooled: It's not broken beyond repair! If educators take even a fraction of Kevin Butler's tenacity, his innovation, and his forward thinking, we'll start making some serious changes within our profession.

—**Joe "Mr. D" Dombrowski**, comedian, speaker, and educator

I met Kevin in 2019 and was blown away by his presence and passion for education. When he shared that he desired to write a book, I knew it would be spectacular. Kevin Butler exceeds all expectations in this instant classic! It's a book you'll want to read again and again. I am inspired and encouraged, ignited and energized.

—**Alicia Ray**, educator, speaker, and author of *Educational Eye Exam*

A pure delight to read! Kevin's exuberance for education and his students shines on every page. *Lights, Cameras, TEACH!* is chock-full of creative tips, games, and innovative ideas that are sure to foster excitement and facilitate a new joy (and camaraderie) in any classroom. This book is a blueprint on how we grow a better community: through creative education, active love, and a shared passion for our future: the children.

—**Jonathan Stutzman**, author of the Tiny T. Rex series, *Llama Destroys the World*, *Bear Is a Bear*, and more

Lights, Cameras, TEACH!

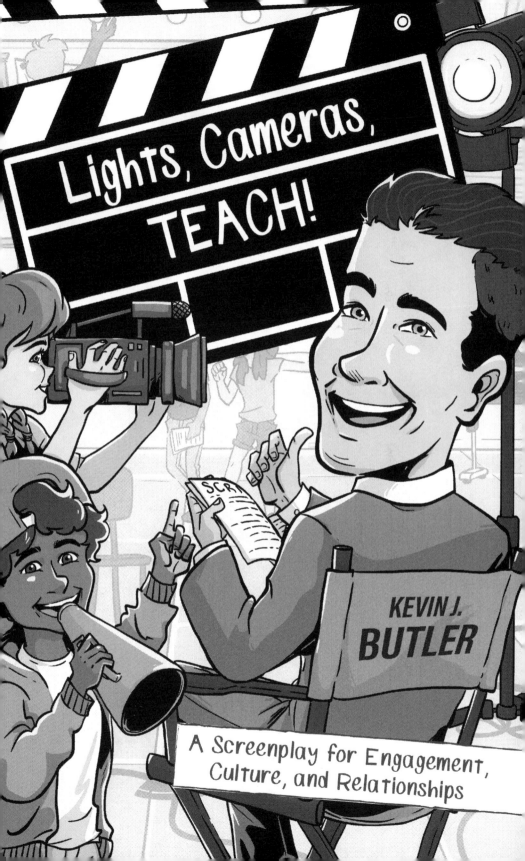

Lights, Cameras, TEACH!

KEVIN J. BUTLER

A Screenplay for Engagement, Culture, and Relationships

Lights, Cameras, TEACH!: A Screenplay for Engagement, Culture, and Relationships
© 2022 Kevin J. Butler

This book is available at special discounts when purchased in quantity for educational purposes or for use as premiums, promotions, or fundraisers. For inquiries and details, contact the publisher at books@daveburgessconsulting.com.

Published by Dave Burgess Consulting, Inc.
San Diego, CA
DaveBurgessConsulting.com

Library of Congress Control Number: 2022943025
Paperback ISBN: 978-1-956306-33-0
Ebook ISBN: 978-1-956306-34-7

Cover art by Yayira Dzamesi
Interior design by Liz Schreiter
Edited and produced by Reading List Editorial
ReadingListEditorial.com

This book is dedicated to the teachers I had the privilege of learning from and who inspired me to follow in their footsteps.

To everyone who gave me a chance (and sometimes a second chance).

To my mom and dad, my former and future students, and to the colleagues and parents who have become some of my closest friends.

To incredible educators everywhere who are making a difference, one student at a time.

To people who are okay with being different and choose not to settle for the status quo simply because it is easier.

And finally, to you. Thank you for being part of a dream I've had since I first walked into a bookstore that someday I would have a book on a bookstore shelf that someone would choose to read.

CONTENTS

Foreword. 1

Preface 5

Introduction: *La La Land*: How I Got Here. 7

Act I: UNITING THE CAST

Chapter One: *Indiana Jones and the Raiders of the Lost Ark*
   Create an Experience. 22

Chapter Two: *Jumanji*
   Make Learning Fun. 51

Act II: ON SET

Chapter Three: *Field of Dreams*
   Classroom Culture 73

Chapter Four: *Akeelah and the Bee*
   Relationships Matter 91

Chapter Five: *Mary Poppins*
   Beyond the Classroom Walls. 109

Chapter Six: *Coach Carter*
   Routines, Procedures, and Expectations 120

Act III: DISTRIBUTION

Chapter Seven: *Willy Wonka and the Chocolate Factory*
   Classroom Design 132

Chapter Eight: *Meet the Parents*
   Parents 144

Chapter Nine: *The Swiss Family Robinson*
   Colleagues 166

Chapter Ten: *Mission Impossible*
    Administrators. 181
Epilogue: *The Mask*
    Lessons from a Pandemic 193

Acknowledgments. 206
Resources and References 208
About the Author 213
More from Dave Burgess Consulting, Inc. 215

Foreword

If you're reading these words, there's a great chance you are deeply invested in the world of education. Possibly you are a teacher, administrator, or parent. Regardless of your role or years of experience, you've likely yearned for innovative ways to increase student engagement, enhance school culture, and perfect stakeholder relationships. Trust me, I get it. As a middle school teacher, former elementary administrator, and the mother of a teenager, I've felt the simultaneous waves of enthusiasm and frustration. And if you, too, have found yourself wading in the water or are seeking proactive measures to avoid it, you've come to the right place. My educator pal, Kevin Butler, has created a masterpiece that is sure to light an uncontainable fire within you.

Before you embark on this journey of self-reflection and creative exploration, I must share that my affinity for this book derives from a philosophy developed through twenty years in education, intensive research in higher learning, and my teaching experiences at the Ron Clark Academy. It is a philosophy heavily imbued with the belief that meaningful relationships are the catalyst to spark interest and excitement in the classroom.

I was introduced to Kevin's work during the spring of 2020, a time when health and economic crises had the world riding an emotional roller coaster. Teachers were pulling every rabbit and educational trick from their hats. And more than ever, people were using social media for inspiration and connection. From my narrow perspective at the time, Kevin was simply a West Coast teacher who had gone viral for his sacrificial act of hand-delivering care packages to each of his fifth grade students. Although his work motivated me to remain tenacious while adjusting to a new virtual environment, I didn't understand how much our values aligned until a mutual friend formally introduced us.

During our first conversation, we bonded over '80s and '90s pop culture, television dramas, and the "madness" of middle school. Through it all, every seemingly unrelated topic would lead right back to the classroom. "And that's how I got the idea to teach the lesson on . . . ," he'd say. It was apparent that his love for teaching was an extension of his love for humanity, and he was willing to use every life experience to enhance the classroom experience of his students. As he continued to talk, my mind traveled down memory lane.

Two decades ago, when I finished my first week as a second grade teacher, I was beyond exhausted—what we educators call "teacher tired." I vividly remember staggering from carpool duty to my classroom, closing my door, and sitting in complete silence, wondering how I would survive 175 more days of teaching. After a moment, I began journaling, and somewhere in the middle of the pages, I penned these words: "I must embrace my inner *Sister Act*."

In case you need a refresher, *Sister Act* is a 1992 movie starring Whoopie Goldberg as Deloris, a lounge singer who witnesses a mob murder and is consequently forced to take refuge in a convent, disguising herself as a nun. Needless to say, a life change like this would require major adjustment. In her new role, she embraces the culture of Catholicism and builds relationships with the sisters of the convent, as well as the children in the choir they lead. However, one of the most momentous scenes of the movie unfolds when Deloris combines her soulful talents with the conventions of the convent and transforms the choir from ordinary to extraordinary, leading them to win first place in a national singing competition.

Sure, it sounds a bit removed from the life of an educator, but is it? Every school year, we face the challenge of adapting to a new environment. The brick and mortar that surround you may be the same, but the students, parents, and staff who flow into them bring different backgrounds, personalities, and experiences. As a first-year teacher, I realized I had to become an entertainer of sorts and to rely on others to succeed. But what took me much longer to understand were the intricate components needed to complete the job successfully. That's why *this* book is crucial.

Lights, Cameras, TEACH! will inspire you to dream bigger and make those dreams a reality. One of the best parts of this book is its ability to diagnose issues without feeling prescriptive. I read chapters forgetting I was reading a book: the way Kevin intertwines the familiarity of movies with common classroom experiences and the voices of other educators makes reading feel more like a conversation with friends. Not only that, I walked away with actual lesson plans and ideas to create more.

Kevin is the perfect person to deliver this message. He is seasoned with years of experience yet has the jovial spirit of a new educator. Plus, the most refreshing part is knowing he's writing from the field, and he has all of the receipts! Every word is supported by personal stories of trial and error, as well as multiple moments of success.

Consider this: Educators across the world begin their school years with plans to change the world. Some of us have the support of like-minded individuals, while others are wandering in the educational abyss. But regardless of where you are in this journey, Kevin's ability to articulate a message will guide you to success.

You often hear educators say, "If I can just touch one child, I've made a difference." But why stop there? Instead, embrace the elements of this book and change the lives of many. I know you won't regret it.

Dr. Yvette Ledford
Ron Clark Academy

Preface

I cannot begin this book without thanking educators. I wrote this book during the most challenging time educators have faced in modern memory: the two years after the World Health Organization declared the Covid-19 pandemic. In just a few days, schools worldwide were required to pivot and revolutionize learning for our students.

At the time of publication, according to a poll conducted in January 2022 by the National Education Association, educators are leaving the profession at alarming rates. Many have spent the last two years feeling overwhelmed, unsupported, underpaid, and unappreciated. We have worried about our own health, the mental and physical health of our students, and about our friends and family members. It saddens my heart to see some of the best educators I know deciding to leave the profession. The Covid-19 pandemic shone a light on the disparity of school resources throughout the United States, from town to town and even within postcodes. After two long years, we are learning to live with Covid-19 and moving toward returning to our day-to-day activities. Unfortunately, the crisis crippling the American educational system still needs to be fixed.

I have had the opportunity of working in public, charter, and independent schools. In addition to being a classroom teacher for two decades, I spent the last six years as a school administrator. While I do not have concrete answers for how to fix the problem our nation has with its school system, I wrote this book to share with you my story, my passion for teaching, and why I do what I do.

Wherever you work in our educational system, you have been through trauma caused by teaching through a global pandemic. I hope to spark ideas that will help rekindle or strengthen your love as an educator and help you remember your why. My why has always been about the kids I teach. The time is now for educators to move forward and reclaim our passion for teaching. My students got me through the last two years. If there is only one thing you get from this book, I hope it's this: relationships matter.

INTRODUCTION

La La Land

How I Got Here

So, what's your favorite movie? *Titanic, Black Panther, The Lord of the Rings*? How about your favorite teacher? Everyone remembers their favorite teacher. Ever since third grade, I knew I wanted to be a teacher. I had the best third grade teacher one can imagine. Mrs. Roelofsen's class wasn't only fun; it was captivating. Everything we did in her class was an experience. Almost thirty years later, I can still put myself back into my third grade classroom. Mrs. Roelofsen was a dynamic storyteller. I remember her reading *Mr. Popper's Penguins* to the class as if it were yesterday. Somehow, she transported us into the book. I loved the class aquarium, the salamander tank, and when we hatched chickens and ducks. She taught us songs to remember the continents and oceans and chants to remember our multiplication tables.

What I remember most, though, was that her class wasn't easy. It was the 1980s, long before *rigor* was an educational catchword. I remember rewriting papers more than once because my handwriting was messy. I remember her calling my home because I was misbehaving (she caught me selling candy in the cafeteria during lunch). I remember she cared. She loved her job, and she loved her students.

Mrs. Roelofsen was honest, and we trusted her. She attended my high school graduation, and we kept in touch for many years after.

I was fortunate enough to go to a really good elementary school. So many of the things I do with my own students were things I remember doing when I was a student. I also went back and did my student teaching there, which felt like a boot camp experience, but I learned so much from those four months. I was teamed up with an incredible teacher, Mrs. Bunce, who threw me right into teaching. As nervous as I was, this helped me build immediate rapport with the class, as well as got me comfortable with teaching in front of the class. She was also beloved by the school community, so I had to be good. She kept me on my game.

Student teachers were expected to do everything "real" teachers did. We needed to dress professionally, be there early and stay late, teach, grade lessons, attend school functions, and communicate with parents. While I wouldn't trade the experience for anything in the world, it was grueling, even at twenty-one years old. It was also incredibly fun. Twenty years later, Mrs. Bunce and I still reminisce about our time together—and she still checks up on me.

Apart from a brief sixth grade phase of wanting to be an architect (I was obsessed with Legos), I determined early on that I wanted to be a teacher. Growing up, I made my friends play school and pretended my house was a school building. I would make my friends listen to my lessons, take tests, give them homework, beg my mother to be the cafeteria server and my father to be the principal. I don't know how I kept any friends.

I grew up in the suburbs of New York, out on Long Island. I grew up middle class, in a middle-class neighborhood. During my senior year of high school, I applied to only two colleges—the University of North Carolina and, to appease my parents, St. Joseph's College (now St. Joseph's University), a small liberal arts school in driving distance of my home. I was accepted by both schools. To make a long story short, because I was an only child, my mother didn't want me to go away to college, so she bargained with me. If I stayed home and went to the local college, she'd get me a new car.

Yeah, I chose the car. Looking back, I have no regrets. The educational program was top-notch, which thoroughly prepared me to enter the field of education.

During my final semester of college, I student-taught at my former elementary school with my second grade teacher (a close runner-up for best teacher ever). I remember sitting in my college student-teaching seminar each week and hearing everyone talking about their weekly adventures in the classroom. I was determined to be the first student to land a teaching job, but during the early 2000s in New York, jobs were hard to obtain. Budget cuts meant hiring freezes, and the market was saturated with applicants. I was mailing out (dating myself) résumés like crazy. After interviewing at several schools, primarily for sub positions, early that December, I was called to interview at a school on the eastern end of Long Island. I had never heard of the town before, but after some research, I learned it was a growing suburb that needed teachers.

The assistant principal, Barbara Lassen, conducted the interview. It was probably one of the most upfront and unaffected job interviews I've ever experienced. She was (and still is) so kind. As I sat in her office, Barbara took the time to look through the portfolio I'd spent weeks making and pointed out things she liked. She was only a few years older than me, and we connected instantly (although we had attended rival high schools). She walked me around the school, introducing me to students and other teachers and staff members. I was no longer nervous, and for a short time, I actually forgot I was on a job interview.

A few days later (after checking my references), Barbara called and offered me a job. I eagerly accepted it. The job was for a fourth grade leave replacement, since the teacher I would be replacing had been in a terrible car accident on her way home from school. I taught her fourth graders for the rest of that school year. I will never forget Barbara's kindness for giving me the chance to pursue my dream.

That first year teaching at Eastport Elementary, I was closer in age to my students than most of the other teachers I worked with at school. Those kids are in their late twenties now, and I still keep in touch with many of them today. But I owe them an apology. I had no idea what I was doing. I can only imagine what their parents thought of me when they met me. I was twenty-two but looked fifteen, and I thought I would change the world. Really, I was just lucky everyone made it to June alive.

Years later, I learned that the principal put the PTA president's child in my class as a mole (to use spy terminology). They wanted someone on the inside who would give honest feedback on my class. A few years later, I taught the PTA president's second son. Today, that son, Kevin, is engaged and finishing up medical school. The elder son, Steven, is a recently married New York City police officer. Eighteen years later, I still get a Christmas card from them, and am in touch with many other members of that class.

Although that first year had been a huge learning experience with many bumps along the way, every child in my class met or exceeded grade-level academic standards in math and reading. At this time, No Child Left Behind was in effect, so test scores were critical to the district office. High test scores meant more state aid. With those good test scores, I'd earned the respect of my principal and the central office.

After several years at this new school, my principal gave me the chance to work with one of my all-time favorite ages: fifth graders. So that year, I looped up several fourth graders to fifth grade. To date, that first-year fifth grade was probably my favorite. It wasn't because the kids were extra smart or well behaved, but rather because the relationships I had already established with these students showed me the power of deep connection with (and knowledge of) our kids. This connection makes all the difference in the world.

This class would come to mean a lot to me, because later that year, my mother died.

In 2003, days after I had accepted my first full-time teaching job, my parents had put my childhood home on the market and moved south to North Carolina. I was devastated. I loved living in New York and had no desire to leave. It saddened me to leave the only home I had ever lived in, but my parents had designed and built their dream home down South. My father loved living in North Carolina while my mother would have preferred to stay in New York. I think my mother hoped that I would move to North Carolina. While I enjoyed visiting them, I never wanted to live there. My parents made new friends, lived in a beautiful neighborhood, and were enjoying their retirement. And then, in October 2008, my mother called me to tell me she had been diagnosed with stage four cancer. The six months between October of 2008 and April 2009 were the worst time of my life. Watching a parent die is something I wouldn't wish on anyone.

A week before spring break of 2009, when I was already planning to head down to visit my parents in North Carolina, my father called and said I should probably try to get there sooner. Somehow thinking another week wouldn't matter and that my classroom couldn't survive without me, I told him I couldn't take any additional time off from work but would be there the following week. However, that night, while I was chaperoning our spring dance, I told my principal, Susan Kenny, about the conversation with my dad. She looked at me and said I needed to get in my car and see my mother—right now. This kind principal told me not to worry about anything at school and reminded me that my class would be fine without me and would be there when I returned. Her support mattered. Relationships matter.

I left the following day. When I arrived at my parents' house, my mother was not well, but we were able to talk, and we discussed a lot of things. I'm deeply grateful for that, because so many people do not have the privilege of those final conversations with loved ones. My mother's last words to me were to live my dreams because life is too short. How true. We are all guilty of wishing time forward, but we also must live with the fact that there is no rewind button. I would give anything to have just one more day with my mother, but thanks to that principal, I was able to hear my mother's final words of advice.

The next day, my mother became incoherent. And three long weeks later, she died. I come from a tiny family, and it was my colleagues, students, and their families who got me through those terrible weeks. I couldn't leave the house, and when I did, I was scared I would return home to find out my mother had passed. The same went for sleeping; neither my dad nor I got much sleep during those three weeks.

Nearly my entire class of fifth graders and their families attended my mother's funeral, which was held back in New York. The comfort of seeing their faces meant more to me than I could ever express in words. I had been away from work for about five weeks and desperately looked forward to getting back to the school. I needed to be around my students and colleagues more than ever. Relationships matter.

A few months later, in the fall of 2009, I had the privilege of visiting the Ron Clark Academy for the first time. If you don't know, the Ron Clark Academy (RCA) is a highly acclaimed not-for-profit independent school in Atlanta, Georgia. RCA has received national and international recognition for its success in creating a loving, dynamic learning environment that promotes academic excellence and leadership. Its students represent various socioeconomic and academic backgrounds and communities from across Atlanta.

Both Ron Clark and Kim Bearden created the school. Not only are they the school's founders, they are also RCA teachers. And RCA isn't just an incredible school, it's also a teacher training center, a place where visiting educators engage in a vibrant professional development experience by observing best practices in action before participating in hands-on workshops led by some of the best educators in the world.

I joined about fifty other educators for a day of professional development. I didn't know a lot about the school, as it had recently opened, but I did remember reading Ron Clark's *New York Times* best-selling book, *The Essential 55*. There are few moments in your life when you can pinpoint the exact moment in time when your life changes, but

Kim Bearden's language arts classroom changed my life. Not only did I get to observe her teaching, I was also able to experience her professional development workshop.

While I *loved* working at Eastport Elementary, I experienced a few difficulties with a handful of colleagues who seemed to dislike the fact that I taught more than just the standards and that I built authentic relationships with my students. As a teacher, I am often perplexed why excellent teachers get the cold shoulder or sometimes even ostracized for being passionate. I cannot think of another profession where the best in the field are asked to tone it down, do less, dim their light, and in some cases, asked to leave.

Well, on that autumn day in 2009, as I listened to Kim's words, relief ran through my body and deep into my soul. Without knowing it, Kim validated the work I was doing. She explained that it was okay to pour your life into your lessons. She affirmed everything I always questioned about myself. Was I too much? Should I tone it down? No.

Kim's words changed the way I looked at my teaching career. I could easily have stayed in my New York classroom, closed the door, and spent the next twenty years doing the same thing. If I'd never heard Kim speak that day—or had not listened so intently to my mother's final words to me—five years later, I probably never would have accepted my job in Los Angeles. I will forever be thankful to Kim Bearden. For everyone who is reading this, please know that blowing out your candle isn't going to make anyone else's shine brighter.

In the early spring of 2014, a start-up charter school in Los Angeles contacted me and made a unique offer to join their faculty as both a consultant and a founding teacher. The school was expanding from K–4 to K–5. I would be a founding fifth grade teacher.

I had spent many summer, winter, and spring breaks in California and, with the help of social media, had also begun connecting with teachers around the United States. Before I knew it, I was connecting with teachers in Los Angeles. After some conversations with the principal of that start-up charter, I visited the school, did a demonstration lesson, and was interviewed by a panel of teachers. Over the next few weeks, the conversations continued.

As terrible as watching my mother die had been, it changed my view of life. I truly realized how short life can be. I never would have accepted that job in California if I hadn't talked with my mother (and received the thumbs-up from my father). I didn't tell many people about my plan to move to California until every *i* was dotted and *t* was crossed.

I owned a house in New York. At the very end of May 2014, I officially signed a contract with the start-up school. By the first of June, my house was listed on the real estate market, and that first day I received an offer for the full asking price. That was the "Oh, crud" moment. I hadn't told my school anything, and only two colleagues (whom I needed as references) knew this was happening. I had a stipulation in my contract with the start-up charter school stating that if my school in New York didn't grant me a one-year leave of absence, I would be unable to commit. I was not keeping this a secret to be shady. Instead, I was nervous—well, probably, more scared. I was terrified!

One day in the school parking lot, a colleague joked around and asked if I was quitting when she saw me filling my car with boxes. I laughed and continued putting those boxes in my car for the next two weeks until my classroom was bare. I wound up moving more classroom supplies to California than I did personal items.

That first week in June, I sent an email to my principal and superintendent requesting a brief meeting. Within minutes, I got a response asking what was going on and saying we could meet now. I walked downstairs to the principal's office. I loved my principal; Sal Alaimo was and still is a role model. He was a fantastic leader (I will write more about that later), and I knew telling him would not be easy. When I walked in, he looked right at me and asked, "Are you leaving?" It was only a guess, but he was right. I explained it all, and to make a long story short, he gave me his full support. He expedited my request for a leave of absence, and on the following Tuesday, the board of education graciously approved my leave of absence.

That type of leave was unprecedented. People thought I was crazy! I was leaving a tenured job at an excellent school, where I made a competitive salary. Over a decade, I had earned enough respect from the administration to run my classroom how I thought was best. I was our building's union representative, an executive member of our school's PTO, and sat on our school district PLC board. I loved my students and their families. The next school year, I would have had an entire class of siblings of former students (which would have been pretty cool). But the stars had aligned, and I had to jump. As my principal had explained to me before, I had my success. It was time to venture into the world and try something new. He reminded me that Eastport Elementary would still be there if I wanted to come back.

I told my class four days before the last day of school. At the end of each school year, I have a special award ceremony for my students and parents at our house banquet. After handing out the awards, I jumped on top of a desk and began to recite a speech I had carefully memorized the night before that would explain everything. I don't think I got past the first sentence before the tears starting streaming. My students began crying. Their parents started crying. Soon, news of my departure spread like wildfire. Now there was no going back.

Los Angeles

That first year living in Los Angeles wasn't what I had envisioned. A week after moving to LA, I suddenly regretted it. I had decided (ignoring the advice of my friends) to live with a roommate. As someone who'd never had a roommate, I should have known better. Not only did I not enjoy sharing a two-bedroom apartment with a stranger, the entire experience was a nightmare. I could write an entire book about my first ten months living in Los Angeles, but I've done my best to forget those horrors.

For the first time in my life, I called my dad each night sobbing about how much I hated it. I was alone in a city that I found wasn't the most welcoming to newcomers. Friends and families of former students came to visit me, and finally I reached out to my school in New York to seriously discuss ending my leave of absence early and returning in January. When I shared that with my father, he encouraged me to stay and reminded me that I'd made a commitment to the school in Los Angeles; if I still was miserable in June, I could go home then.

Work was the only safe place: I had a great group of kids and parents who were extremely supportive. Several colleagues became my friends and therapists, and then, slowly, I made friends outside of work and began to acclimate to LA.

So, that one-year leave of absence turned into two years. And while I learned a lot during my two years at the start-up school, and the intentions of the school were good, it honestly wasn't a fit and that was okay. Also, if you've never worked at a start-up school, it's a lot of work! Budgets were tight, resources were extremely limited, and the school didn't have a permanent campus. I had been planning on returning to New York but realized I'd fallen in love with the Southern California lifestyle. It's 75 degrees and sunny every day! I remember a February day when I got in my car after having dinner, thinking how cold it was. When I looked down at my dashboard, the temperature read 62 degrees. Back home, they were shoveling themselves out of a blizzard. When did 62 degrees become cold? By this time, I had made some good friends and was happily living alone.

With a few months left to decide if I was returning to my job in New York or staying in California, I began to interview for teaching positions all over the Los Angeles County.

At the last minute—before having to either return to my job in New York or resign—I was asked to interview at a small, independent school only a ten-minute drive from my home. The school's founder interviewed me. He had started the school as a one-room schoolhouse with a mission focused on the total child almost sixty-five years earlier. He asked me the best questions, all related to kids and learning. Questions like, "Why do you like teaching?" "What do you like to teach?" and "Who was your favorite teacher and why?" I was then interviewed by the head of school and was given a tour of the campus. I was introduced to kids, staff members, and teachers. I met the other fifth grade teacher, Mary Chen. Without question, I knew I wanted to work with her. I think it's rare to bond with someone so quickly. In a matter of an hour, we talked about everything from curriculum to our favorite movies. We jibed. It was a friends-at-first-sight kind of thing. I had found a new partner in crime. After a demonstration lesson and another school visit, I was offered and accepted a job to teach fifth grade and to also become the school's coordinator for curriculum and instruction. Relationships matter.

Lights, Cameras, TEACH!

October 2019. A teacher (me) walks into a bar (really). I was presenting at the Teach Better 19 Conference in Akron, Ohio. I didn't know anyone. Somehow, I managed the courage to walk up to a table and introduce myself to Adam Welcome. For those who may not know who Adam Welcome is, Adam is a longtime educator. He has served as a teacher, principal, and a director of innovation in the San Francisco Bay region. He has authored four educational books and is a phenomenal public speaker who motivates educators to be their best. Adam was the keynote speaker for the conference. It was the first time I had presented at a large conference, the first time I was in Ohio, and the first time I was meeting several of my teacher idols. Thinking back, that bar was packed with teacher icons. Adam Welcome, Shelley and Dave Burgess, Rae Hughart, Becky Schnekser, Alicia Ray, Jonathan Stamper, Allyson Apsey, Tara Martin—the list goes on and on. And at the time, I knew none of them personally.

Adam asked me for my Twitter handle, and I told him I barely use Twitter. He looked at me and told me to log onto my account. I couldn't remember my password. After a few tries, I logged in. Adam tweeted out to his personal learning network (PLN) that I was joining the Twitter world and was in need of some followers. In less than an hour, I had a thousand new Twitter friends.

Also, Adam gave me some good advice. For years I'd been told to write a book, but that's easier said than done. First, Adam told me that anyone can write a book. If I was serious about getting a book published, he said, then I needed to spend the time laying the groundwork.

A week or so later, I was back home in Los Angeles, driving home in rush-hour traffic on the 101, when my phone rang. I answered it, and it was Adam. Adam Welcome, calling me? He was checking in on my Twitter progress (I swear I am not smart enough to navigate the intricacies of Twitter). Then, he asked more about my book idea and what I was going to do to accomplish my goals of getting it published. I made it clear that I only wanted one person to publish this book, Dave Burgess Consulting. Period. And then I listened very carefully to what Adam told me. Over the next two years, I did everything he suggested that day. I connected with educators from around the world, I created my own PLN, I blogged, hosted a (short-lived) podcast, presented my material at more conferences (even in the middle of a global pandemic), moderated Twitter chats, and updated a very antiquated website. If Adam was watching, I wasn't going to disappoint.

Finally, in the summer of 2021, I became serious about writing. I had a good outline, a handful of chapters drafted,. When the world began to open back up, I was able to start traveling again. I started my summer visiting Nashville, Tennessee, a city that's been on my bucket list for years. I loved Nashville. I don't think there is anywhere else you can walk down a street and have so much live music at your fingertips. Every establishment on Broadway was packed (this was on a Monday night, too) with multiple floors of live musicians playing. The people were friendly, and the food was delicious.

From there, I went to Atlanta, Georgia. My friend Kim Bearden invited me to help her celebrate the release of her newest book, *Fight*

Song. While I was there, I also got to spend two days at my one of my favorite spots in the world: the Ron Clark Academy. On the evening of Kim's book party, Ron came up to me and told me he heard that I was writing a book and told me it was about time. Was I imagining this? This couldn't be real. He liked the synopsis, and it was his idea to title each chapter after a blockbuster movie.

So, since this is my own *True Hollywood Story*, I will be spilling some behind-the-scenes tea throughout. The purpose of this book is to tell my story, as well as give you an insider's look into my two decades as a classroom teacher. I've had the privilege to work in three very different settings: a suburban public school, an urban charter school, and an independent school in the suburbs of a metropolis. Over my years as a teacher, I've also been able to create relationships with some incredible educators, many who helped mold me into the educator I am today.

Directing and Teaching: Creating Communities, Guiding Experiences

DIRECTORS

Directors are the creative leads on a movie set. They hold the creative vision throughout the whole process, from preproduction through to the final edit. Directors are employed by the producer, who is ultimately in charge of a production. Directors direct the making of a film by visualizing the script while guiding the actors and technical crew to capture the vision for the screen. Directors control the film's dramatic and artistic aspects and are in charge of the outcome of the film.

Well, let's compare that to our roles as classroom teachers:

TEACHERS

Teachers are the creative leads in their classrooms. They hold the creative vision throughout the whole process, from the first day of school through the last day. Teachers are employed by the school, which is in charge of distributing the curriculum. Teachers direct the execution of the curriculum by visualizing the content while guiding the students and parents to capture the tone of the year. Teachers control the class's academic and social-emotional well-being and are in charge of the outcomes for their students.

A blockbuster movie needs more than a director to become a blockbuster. It needs a producer, writers, actors, stagehands, and sometimes even codirectors. All of these people work together with a common goal: to create that blockbuster movie. Directors work hard to build relationships with everyone on their set because they know that is the only way to achieve their vision. As teachers, we must work with everyone, reaching out not just to our students but to their parents, our colleagues, administrators, and staff to build relationships that support our own vision of a successful classroom community.

My hope is that the stories, lessons, and resources I share throughout this book will help spark ideas for your own classroom. My goal is to inspire fellow educators and get teachers to open their classroom doors and invite others into their spaces to see their classroom story. Throughout my own story here, I will be sharing the voices of my former students and those of educators from around the United States. Please steal, borrow, tweak, and share what you liked reading and use it to help you direct your own blockbuster. At the end of each chapter, I have included what I call "Action" pages. Use these pages to reflect or—if you are utilizing this book as a grade-level or school-wide read for professional development—use them as group discussion starters.

Act I

UNITING THE CAST

CHAPTER ONE

Indiana Jones and the Raiders of the Lost Ark

Create an Experience

*I*ndiana Jones and the Raiders of the Lost Ark was one of my favorite action movies growing up and is my favorite ride at Disneyland. Both are full of twists and turns, surprises and action! When walking into my classroom, you will see students in action. What are they doing? Well, that depends on the day. I believe that students should be active participants in their learning, and the teacher's role should be that of facilitator. A facilitator helps engage others in meaningful discussion while also being an active participant. When students are engaged, not only will they learn but they are more likely to remember what they learned.

The term *active learning* comes from educator Edgar Dale's research, which states that we humans remember 90 percent of what we do. On social media, I often share immersion lessons called *room simulations*. These simulations take a lesson and make a learning experience out of it, with the ultimate goal being to create an environment of active learning.

Kids today are born being entertained. From the time they enter the world, there's entertainment everywhere. While as teachers we didn't train to be entertainers, our teaching must capture students' attention and, yes, at times entertain them. This does not mean that every lesson must be a Broadway musical number, but it should mean that we are intentional when engaging our students in active learning. In Dave Burgess's book *Teach Like a Pirate*, Dave discusses creating lessons that your students would buy a ticket to participate in. I love being able to transport my students into an experience they won't forget. I call these experiences *lesson simulations*, and I do one for every major topic of study I teach.

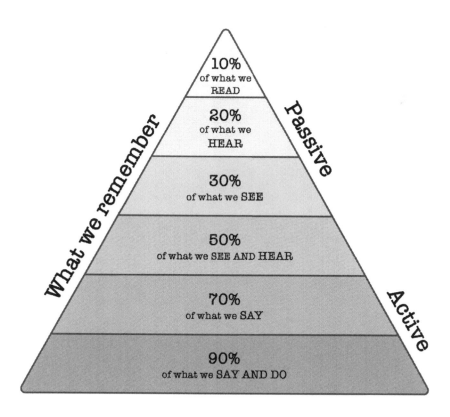

Dale's cone shows that "action learning" techniques result in up to 90 percent retention. People learn best when engaged in perceptual learning styles. Perceptual learning styles are sensory based. The more interaction with a topic, the better chance that many students will be able learn from it. According to Dale, instructors should consistently design activities that build upon real-life experiences. In my simulation lessons, I try to submerse my students in an experience that incorporates as many parts of Dale's cone as possible.

Lesson Simulations Include:

1. Text(s) for students to read
2. Students gathering information from listening (including from their peers)
3. Use of images or videos
4. Hands-on or interactive activities
5. Aspects from "the real world"
6. A purposeful experience, such as role-playing or collaboration
7. Direct alignment with content standards

It's important that we as educators create a sense of urgency in our classrooms from day one. While not every lesson needs to be high energy, all of them should be engaging. Students will learn quickly that every minute we spend together at school is meaningful. This sets the stage for the importance of paying attention, as students know everything we do has impact. The goal should be to have students sitting on the edges of their seats, waiting to hear what they are going to do next.

Many of the students in our classrooms need extra time. For students who do need that extra time, or who need reteaching, I have built in time in our schedule called *priority work time*. This is dedicated time in our daily schedule for students to work on ongoing assignments. And because my class is fast-paced, I use this time to work with students in small groups or one-on-one, making sure they understand by answering their questions or by reteaching the material. This is also a valuable time to use for students who benefit from pre-teaching or post-teaching review. Priority work time normalizes the idea that not everyone learns at the same pace.

You might not be able to implement every lesson and idea I share in this book, but I hope to spark ideas that you can use in your own classroom. Also think of this book as taking a trip to a big box store. While it's very tempting to buy everything the store has, we can't fit all of that into our shopping cart. We choose what we need and want to take home with us.

An example: On any given weekend, you can find me visiting my favorite plant shops to see what new plants they are carrying. I love houseplants. As much as I want almost all of them, I can't take them all home. So, what I do is browse. That's what I hope you'll do with the ideas in this book. Browse. Think about what you can try. Maybe it's just a piece of a lesson, a resource, wearing a costume, or playing a new game. Teachers are always borrowing ideas from other teachers. The best lessons we have in our toolbox were most likely inspired by something we saw or experienced. Take my ideas and make them yours.

While you may not be teaching the same content I am, think about what you teach and how you can create a learning *experience* for your students.

Indiana Jones and the Lost City

While real archaeologists do not raid tombs, snatch golden idols, or fall into booby-trapped chambers, *Indiana Jones* was the perfect backdrop for a lesson on ancient civilizations. Students come to class and simulate the experience of being an archaeologist. In addition to hitting social science standards, this lesson incorporates language arts standards, including both inferencing and summarizing.

Student Voice: Being Taught by Indy

My favorite memory was all the room transformations, specifically *Indiana Jones*. This was one of our first room transformations, and I remember how awesome it was. We walked into the new room with cave-like wallpaper, activities, and Mr. Butler dressed up as Indiana Jones! I remember discovering a necklace! The overall memory was of the excitement in the room, the effort involved, and being able to brag to other classes about what I experienced in class.

Hudson, class of 2020

Before students arrive, I fill extra-large plastic containers with sand and carefully bury artifacts (a mix of miniature items and laminated pictures). Students rotate around the classroom completing various tasks. One task is for students to read an article on archaeology. In addition to reading, students practice answering comprehension questions and defining vocabulary words. When students join at the excavation site, they put on their hard hats, gather their digging tools, and begin carefully digging for artifacts.

As students uncover an artifact, they return to their desks and write in their archaeology journals. First, they describe the artifact they found, focusing on what natural resource it may have been made from. Second, they infer what the artifact may have been used for. After everyone has found and analyzed an artifact, we compile a list of all the artifacts they uncovered.

Through guided writing, we write a summary describing what life may have been like in this lost city. For example, students infer that since someone found a necklace made from shells, the city must have been located near a large body of water. A gold coin may have been used for trading, and a bow and arrow could be evidence that these people hunted animals.

When students finish, they use a *Kids Discover* magazine to dig deeper (no pun intended) into learning about what archaeologists do and reflect on their experiences as archaeologists.

Materials:

1. Large plastic container
2. Play sand
3. Small artifacts (objects or laminated photos)
4. *Kids Discover* magazine, *Archaeology* issue
5. Plastic hard hats, decorations (optional)

Cost: $$
Prep time: 60–75 minutes prior to the lesson
Lesson duration: One or two periods (60–75 minutes)
Players: Mostly independent
Supporting players: Teacher helps students "dig" for artifacts
ELL support: Pre-teach vocabulary; use sentence frames to help students write their summary

A Cruise Around the World

In two weeks, we are going on our first field trip—a cruise around the world—and I don't want to have to call any of your parents to tell them you've been lost at sea . . . .

That's how I begin the unit on world geography. I inform students that we will be going on a cruise and that it is vital they have map skills, especially an understanding of latitude and longitude.

Two weeks later, my students arrive in class to see me dressed up as a ship captain. I collect each student's ticket and allow them to board the cruise ship. To their surprise, the entire classroom has been turned into a cruise ship. Seagulls hang from the ceiling, oceans sounds play in the background, and giant backdrops of the ocean horizon disguise the walls.

Students are handed sunglasses and Hawaiian leis to wear, and then must use latitude and longitude coordinates throughout the simulation to plot the locations our cruise ship visits. I place giant maps on tables, and students work collaboratively with a partner to keep track of their travels in a travel journal. Each student is provided with a list

of coordinates they must plot on their map. Each coordinate is a city (located on a body of water), and each city is labeled with a Post-it note. When students think they have successfully made it to the last stop, I go over to check that they have plotted each city correctly. Students then complete two different activities: one is to read a passage on Newsela about Gladys West and her contribution to the creation of GPS; the other is to read a *Kids Discover* magazine on maps and globes. Both resources come with comprehension activities that students can work on. This also allows me to support students who may need additional help or time to complete the task of plotting the points on their map.

Materials:

1. World maps (oversized maps from Lakeshore Learning; I suggest laminating them so you can reuse)
2. *Kids Discover* magazine, *Maps and Globes* issue
3. Newsela article: "Gladys West"
4. Post-it notes
5. Plastic leis, sunglasses, decorations (optional)

Cost: $

Prep time: 30–60 minutes prior to the lesson

Lesson duration: One period (45–60 minutes)

Players: Pairs or trios

Supporting players: Teacher check-in. Optional: parent volunteers, co-teachers.

ELL support: Allow students to work in cooperative pairs to promote communication and teamwork.

Our Cruise Around the World

Stop 1 - Mapping Coordinates

Stop 2 - Kids Discover Magazine

Stop 3 - Gladys West and GPS

Stop 4 - Design Your Own Map!

5a - due Monday 10/4
5b - due Tuesday 10/5
5c - due Wednesday 10/6

Mr. Butler's Cruise Around the World
A Mapping Simulation

The Reading King

I just can't wait to be king!

That's what I tell my students to open our unit on nonfiction text features. During this unit, I invite students to join me on a text-feature safari. The Reading King simulation is one of my favorites because it's inspired by my favorite animated film, *The Lion King*. On this reading safari, students try to find different nonfiction text features we've learned about. Each student is supplied with a travel magazine, a safari survival pack (a bag of dried fruit, a small bottle of water, and a mechanical pencil). They wear safari hats and use binoculars to find text features throughout the magazine. As students find these text features, they annotate their safari guide. In addition to animal sounds playing in the background, I place giant three-dimensional cardboard

safari animals (from Amazon) around the classroom and backdrops of the African savannah cover the walls.

Students also receive a text-feature guide to help them both identify and explain the various text features that may be found in their magazine. Students identify as many text features (headings, subheading, drawings, maps, pictures, bold-print words, etc.) in the magazine as possible. In addition to listing each text-feature they find, they focus on one article and summarize that article.

Materials:

1. Assorted magazines (ask your school or local library for copies of old magazines)
2. Text-feature guide (teacher created)
3. Plastic safari hats (hard hats from the archaeology simulation), props, decorations (optional), sound effects

Cost: $

Prep time: 30–60 minutes prior to the lesson

Lesson duration: One period (45–60 minutes)

Players: Independent or pairs

Supporting players: Teacher check-in

ELL support: Provide students with sentence frames to help write their article summary.

Grammarcraft

The only thing I knew about *Minecraft* was that my students were *obsessed* with it.

One year, we were just finishing up learning about the parts of speech in grammar and I decided to make a simulation based on the game. In our version, called Grammarcraft, students built sentences using different parts of speech they'd learned with the help of Flocabulary's "Parts of Speech" rap.

Throughout our entire grammar unit, students had become accustomed to color coding each part of speech they were using when writing sentences. For Grammarcraft, I took the same color-coding system and printed various parts of speech out on colored paper—nouns on purple, verbs on red, conjunctions on yellow, and so on. Students cut out words and "build" sentences using as many parts of speech as possible. As students create their sentences, they glue them down into their grammar notebook and then label each word with its part of speech.

Materials:

1. Colored copy paper (a different color for each part of speech)
2. Glue sticks
3. Flocabulary video (optional)
4. Notebook or lined paper
5. *Minecraft* decorations (optional)

Cost: $

Prep time: 45–60 minutes prior to the lesson

Lesson duration: One period (45–60 minutes)

Players: Independent or pairs

Supporting players: Teacher check-in.

ELL support: Create sentences with blanks and have students focus on filling in the blanks rather than building entire sentences. If possible, include examples in the students' native language(s).

Educator Spotlight:
Rounding = Classroom Fun? Yes!

Rounding was always the first thing we taught in third grade. There was a lesson in the very first manual. Despite spending a ton of time working on this skill and all the spiral reviews I did, by March, they had a tendency to forget it. I remembered Dave Burgess saying, "Provide an uncommon experience for your students, and they will reward you with an uncommon effort and attitude." Game on!

The week before our state testing, I put together Hungry Hungry Hippos, math-style. I placed students into groups of a variety of academic levels and provided instructions. On the hippo "food"—small plastic balls, similar to what you would find in a childrens' ball pit—were labels with numbers. In the first round, one student was on a scooter (free of charge, thanks to our PE teacher), while another student pushed and pulled them as they tried to capture hippo food with their "nest" (a laundry basket). As a team, students first added the numbers on their captured food and rounded to the nearest tens and hundreds, doing their work on small whiteboards. In the second round, they rounded first and then added, and in the third round, rounded and then subtracted.

I allowed our class one full period to accomplish this, but something magical happened: The students were helping each other and showing the bonds they had built over the year. They were

excited to round and do math. Needless to say, one period turned into three, and students said they had the best day ever. It did not take much to create this event, but I know it created a lasting memory.

Amanda Mast,
teacher and principal
@amanda_mast0325

Rodeo Roundup

Your homework tonight is to come to math class tomorrow with boots, because my farmer friend is dropping off two hundred pigs that we need to round up and organize. If anyone is afraid of getting messy, I will give you a worksheet to work on next door.

After teaching students about rounding decimals, I do a Rodeo Roundup room simulation in which students become "ranchers" and must collect pigs branded with numbers that will round to a number they have been assigned.

For this lesson, in addition to being dressed as a farmer, I have pig sounds playing in the background and a big red barn backdrop covering the wall. The night before this lesson, I stay after school and blow up about two hundred pink balloons, enough for each of my twenty-four students (working in collaborative pairs) to collect eight

balloon pigs. I make a combination of large balloons and small balloons to represent "big pigs" and "baby pigs," then I write a number on each balloon. These will round to the number each pair of students is assigned. For example, a student may have a box that I labeled with numbers. One box may be labeled 0.564. The student must search the classroom for eight "pigs" branded with numbers that will round to 0.564, such as 0.5641 or 0.5639. After students find two big pigs and six baby pigs, they bring their box of pigs to me. I check over their work to see if they "rounded up" the correct pigs.

Now, these pigs do not need to be created from balloons. I have also done this using printed pictures of pigs with decimals written on each picture. Kids still get the experience of searching for pigs that would round to their assigned number, and this holds their interest much better than a page from a math workbook! I've also seen teachers take this idea and do it with antonyms and synonyms, multiplication and division, and various phonics patterns, all to great effect.

Materials:

1. Pink balloons or pig clipart on paper
2. Cardboard boxes or large grocery-style paper bags
3. Student worksheets
4. Clipboards (optional)

Cost: $

Prep time: 60–90 minutes prior to the lesson

Lesson duration: One period (30–45 minutes)

Players: Cooperative pairs

Supporting players: Teacher check-in

ELL support: Include visuals in addition to words and numbers on their roundup boxes or bags.

Student Voice:
Perfectly Fitted Learning Styles

Learning styles are like clothing: there are many different colors, styles, and sizes, and in most scenarios, a one-size-fits-all outfit doesn't truly fit everyone. I struggled a lot with learning when I was younger, but in fifth grade, Mr. Butler opened a path to success for me by showing me I could combine music with school in order to learn. I remember how he took songs and adapted them to help us study. I can still recite those songs perfectly today, eight years later, because of the impact they had on my life. Every teacher should strive to make learning fun and different so students around the world can find an "outfit" that works for them.

Emily, class of 2012

Back to the Future

Tomorrow, I will not be able to make it to school, but my friend Mr. Hamilton will be in to cover class. I expect everyone to help him out as he teaches.

My goal when teaching American history is to present content from multiple perspectives. I think it's so important for students to be able to not just think critically, but to be able to see things, like history, from multiple perspectives. This does not mean that students need to agree with each viewpoint, but that they can develop an understanding that there is often more than one way to see something. A perfect introduction to this is to show students pictures of various optical illusions. I ask students to write down what they see and then we share their responses. Students are often mind-blown when they are able to see both images, that sometimes there is no clear right or wrong answer.

At the beginning of my American Revolution unit, I transform my classroom into Independence Hall. In my Back to the Future lesson, I take students back in time to Philadelphia, Pennsylvania, to learn the perspectives of colonial patriots and English loyalists.

While sipping tea, eating biscuits (cookies), and wearing spectacles, students read four different articles (by battery-operated candlelight). Students take notes using a quill pen (ballpoint pens that I hot-glue feathers to) inside a leatherbound (pleather) journal as we analyze primary and secondary sources.

For this lesson, we use various song lyrics from Lin-Manuel Miranda's *Hamilton* as well as written words from Samuel Seabury's *Free Thoughts, on the Proceedings of the Continental Congress* and Alexander Hamilton's *A Full Vindication for the Measures of Congress*. I dress up as both Alexander Hamilton and King George, while we analyze these sources so students can distinguish between the viewpoints of both groups of people.

Materials:

1. Song lyrics
2. Hamilton curriculum from the Gilder Lehrman Institute (free)
3. T-chart (copies for each student)
4. Costumes, decorations (optional)

Cost: $

Prep time: 30–60 minutes prior to the lesson

Lesson duration: Two periods (60–120 minutes)

Players: Whole class/partner share

Supporting players: Teacher facilitates discussion

ELL support: Preview vocabulary with students ahead of time. Provide students with definitions of words that are vital to understanding these challenging texts.

Text Structure Madness

What's March Madness all about, anyway?

In March I introduce students to the college basketball tournament by inviting them to read and listen to information about it on the excellent learning website Wonderopolis. I then incorporate March Madness into part of our nonfiction unit in March, when students will participate in a game of Text Structure Madness. After a class discussion on the five different nonfiction text structures, I turn the classroom into a college basketball court and divide students into two teams.

Students receive a set of short nonfiction passage task cards, a die, a mini basketball, a whiteboard, and a dry-erase marker. Task cards are just questions printed on paper and cut out into cards. Task cards are easy to find on websites like Teachers Pay Teachers, and for a few dollars, you can often find task cards on any topic you are teaching. Many task cards are created with various ability levels, so differentiation is easy. When I give my students an assignment using task cards, I print them out on card stock.

When the clock starts, students have sixty seconds to read their passages and determine the text structure (compare/contrast, cause/effect, description, sequence, problem/solution). Each player (student) writes their answers down on the whiteboard, and when the timer buzzes, they hold their whiteboards up. The students who answered the question correctly get about thirty seconds or so to shoot their basketball into the basket. The game continues for about thirty minutes, with two team captains keeping score and one point for each basket made.

This game is based on lessons from *The Comprehension Toolkit*, written by Stephanie Harvey and Anne Goudvis. The student passages I purchase and download from Teachers Pay Teachers.

Materials:

1. Task cards (paragraphs on task cards, bound with a binder ring)
2. Basketball net (I buy plastic basketball pails from the dollar store)
3. Miniature basketballs (one for each student) or crumpled-up orange construction paper.
4. Whiteboards and dry-erase markers. Tip: Create whiteboards by inserting a piece of white paper into a page protector.

Cost: $$

Prep time: 30–60 minutes prior to the lesson

Lesson duration: One period (45–60 minutes)

Players: Independent

Supporting players: Teacher acts as referee. Optional: team captains to help tally points.

ELL support: Preview or send passages home with students prior to the game or provide students with a reference chart reminding them of the various text structures and clue words.

The Genre World Series

One, two, three strikes you're out!

During the World Series, I turn my classroom into a baseball field. I simply arrange students' desks into a diamond shape and use green tablecloths and burlap. I hang up a baseball backdrop and place Cracker Jack containers around the room.

Students are paired up and given a small game board to use. One student in each pair takes a bat icon, and the other uses a baseball icon (I print the pictures out and laminate them). Each pair of students receives a pile of task cards with a paragraph printed on it. Students take turns reading the paragraph and must determine the genre. Before this simulation, students will have studied and read various genres of fiction, such as fantasy, science fiction, historical fiction, realistic

fiction, mystery, drama, and adventure. I do this by showcasing various books from our classroom library and creating an anchor chart with each genre's attributes. Over the course of two weeks, students read various passages I've collected from magazines like Scholastic *Storyworks*. During the game, if a student identifies the genre correctly, they roll the dice and score either a single, double, triple, or a home run. The player who has the most "scores" (points) at the end of the game is the winner. While this activity is simple, it's more engaging than a worksheet.

Materials:

1. Genre task cards (printed from Teachers Pay Teachers)
2. Game board (teacher-created baseball diamond)
3. Game pieces
4. Green and brown tablecloths, decorations (optional)

Cost: $

Prep time: 30–45 minutes prior to the lesson

Lesson duration: One period (45–60 minutes)

Players: Pairs or two teams of two

Supporting players: Teacher check-in, optional guest umpire

ELL support: Preview or send passages home with students prior to the game or provide students with a reference chart with the various fiction genres. Add visuals to task cards.

Educator Spotlight:
Converted by Sims

Being Kevin's teaching partner has changed me as an educator. His energy, creativity, and ideas breathed new life through our campus. Being more "traditionalist," room transformations seemed intimidating and time-consuming. So, when Kevin asked me to join him in his Decimals Cafe simulation, I was thrilled to ride his coattails . . . straight into the bakery! I put on my server attire—a hat and matching apron—and was blown away when I entered his classroom. Simply by rearranging desks and adding tablecloths, flower vases, and even place settings, he created instant ambience. I was as in awe of this instant transformation as the kids were oohing and aahing over the experience, enjoy-

ing the little desserts, and admiring the custom menu. It was such a memorable day as both an educator and "patron" of the cafe! Working with him has taught me that creating these little moments is worth the time.

Mary Chen, fifth grade teacher
@jpochen3

Simulation FAQs

The most frequent questions I'm asked about my room simulations are around who pays for all the stuff and where I store it all. These lesson simulations were created over many years. And remember, these are special lessons. It would be impossible for every day in anyone's classroom to be like this.

When I gather materials for my simulations, I have a few tips:

SHOP WISELY.

We are teachers, and we are all on a budget! I usually buy consumable things, like paper, markers, colored pencils, labels, and folders with my classroom budget. I'm very frugal when it comes to buying materials for simulation lessons. Props and decorations that I reuse from year to year I either buy myself or try to get donated. Check out secondhand stores, yard sales, and Craigslist for bargains!

BUY THINGS ON SALE.

I use coupons and teacher discounts whenever possible. If something isn't on sale, I will tell the cashier (in my nicest teacher voice) that I am a teacher, and the materials I am buying will be used in school. Almost always, they will give me a discount. In addition, there's no harm in asking for donations. It's surprising what families may have at home or can get from someone they know.

DonorsChoose is a fantastic resource to get classroom projects funded. Check out their website for information on how you can submit a request for classroom materials. Many of the more expensive items in my classroom were funded with the help of DonorsChoose. You can also post things on your Amazon wish list and have friends, family, and parents of students purchase items off that list. I recently saw teachers posting QR codes of their Amazon wish lists at local businesses (with the owner's permission).

REUSE EVERYTHING.

If you look closely at my photos, you will see the same items used over and over again. The safari hats are also archaeological hats. The green tablecloths from Genre World Series are used for Independence Hall. The sunglasses from the cruise are the same glasses students use for their safari.

BORROW.

I borrow a lot (and lend a lot, too). I borrow from friends, family, other classrooms, and even my own home. My costumes often come from a generous former parent who works in the costume industry and allows me to borrow the costumes at no cost.

COLLABORATE WITH COLLEAGUES.

Team up with another teacher on your grade level or a specialist. One of my less complicated simulations is the Dessert Cafe. In this simulation students enter a fictional cafe and order items off the menu. The task is not only to stick to a budget, but to be able to calculate the tax and tip. I tell students lengthy stories of times when I have been out with friends, and grown adults cannot figure out how much to leave for a tip. The reason why this one of my favorite lessons is that I collaborate with three of my colleagues. I have our music teacher come in and play the piano and the other fifth grade teacher and I become the servers. Our principal becomes the host and brings the diners to their seats. The kids love seeing teachers work together.

STORAGE ISN'T SO EASY.

When I taught in New York, I had a HUGE walk-in closet (the size of a small classroom) to store my materials. I certainly miss that room. Currently, there's only limited storage in my classroom: one small area I hide behind a curtain that fits about eight large bins of materials. The school maintenance team has been very accommodating in helping me find space on campus to store some of my larger props.

USE SOCIAL MEDIA.

Social media is such a fantastic platform to share and gather ideas. I love seeing what other teachers are doing in their classrooms and sharing my lessons and activities.

Educator Spotlight: Creating Experiences

Long before I ever knew any better, I planned new experiences as well as lessons for my students in my very first classroom. It was third grade, and we had a poetry reading in our "Jamestown Cafe." I reset our classroom as a small cafe with snacks and hot chocolate. There was an "open mic" for each student to read their poem. The audience snapped its approval! Dollar Tree was my best friend for supplies. From this, I knew that creating an experience my students would remember was THE way to hook them with lessons.

While teaching fourth grade, on day one, I shared a flight with my students. They received their boarding passes in the hallway. Water and Biscoff cookies were provided as the inflight snack, and a video of my summer vacation created by my husband was the inflight movie. I know this made a huge impact because in the second semester of that year, my students had some practice writing prompts to get ready for the state writing test. One of the prompts asked about a time they remembered from school. Most students wrote about that flight from the first day of school.

My very favorite experience was for the culmination of reading *A Wrinkle in Time*. This was the year the newest movie came out, and students would get to see it after we had finished the book. To review for the comprehension assessment, my teacher bestie, Patti Robinson, and I transformed our classrooms into one of the bizarre planets from the book. We had toddler crawling tubes from IKEA hanging from the ceiling to represent the tesseract that would take us through space and time. Black tablecloths hung on all the walls with some planetary decorations. It looked like we were in space! Patti and I both dressed as Mrs. Whatsit, in costumes we got from thrift shops. You truly don't need to spend a ton of money to do a transformation. When we saw the movie together at the theater, it was incredible to hear the kids make connections to the book and explain when things weren't the same and why they thought that was so. Creating experiences does matter! Learning should be fun! Not every day can be a

room transformation, but every day there can be something a little different and interesting. If we make school a place where kids want to be, that's half the battle. If they are in school, they will learn!

Deb James, middle school teacher
@mayor_james_

ACTION!

1. What's one way you can engage students in active learning in your classroom?
2. What's one "blockbuster" lesson you have taught (or could teach)?
3. Make a list of things or people who have inspired you as a teacher.

CHAPTER TWO

Jumanji

Make Learning Fun

*J*ust as the characters in *Jumanji* needed to carefully navigate between unexpected adventure and a game of survival, teachers need to carefully navigate between making learning fun, while at the same time ensuring we address the required learning content and standards. Learning needs to be fun, but not everything can be a game. And as much as I love my room simulations, remember that those are special lessons. Using games in the classroom is no longer left for "Friday Funday" but is part of my daily instructional practice. There is enormous value in kids participating in educational games to review content as they learn how to work collaboratively. At the same time, we must teach the content standards, differentiate lessons, and keep our instruction rigorous.

For using games to review academic subjects, there are four rules I share with teachers:

1. All students must be active participants. There shouldn't be anyone sitting back just watching or waiting for their turn.
2. Answer keys prevent students from working cooperatively to figure out if they are right or wrong. I should be the last person they ask for help regarding answers to questions about the game.

3. Don't tell students how long the game will last. Not knowing how long a game will last helps to muster a sense of urgency and prevents students from wasting time. Most of the games I play with my students last from three to fifteen minutes. I try to play a game once a week. Playing games too often takes away from it being a special activity.

4. Students should be aware of the academic objective of the game and be able to explain the purpose of the game to anyone who enters the room.

Educator Spotlight: Cross-Discipline Content Creators (with LEGOgraphy)!

One of my favorite activities with young explorers is LEGOgraphy. You can use it across disciplines, grade levels, content areas, or just for fun. I often use it as a way to hook young explorers, connect to a familiar part of their life, and sneak in some content knowledge and assessment opportunities. (That sentence makes it sound boring, but I assure you that it generates some of the most creative experiences with learners.)

LEGOgraphy is the practice of using LEGO minifigures within photography. All you need are LEGO minifigures, and photography can be completed with iPads, Chromebooks, cell phones, or old-school illustrations on paper. This activity can be used in person, remotely, or a combination of those: it is the ultimate utility experience. Using LEGO minifigures, learners create small-scale scenes that can be used for creative writing, illustrating a story, demonstrating scientific concepts—anything your mind can come up with. As a field scientist, I travel with LEGO minifigures and use them to bring the field back to my young explorers, as well as to demonstrate scientific concepts.

For example, while in Galápagos, I wanted to bring back the dramatic sand coloration from the islands and help my explorers see the different sizes, shapes, and textures of sand grains from each of the islands. What better way to do this than to stage photographs on location with a LEGO minifigure that looks like me?

Instant engagement on so many levels, and excitement about doing this type of photography themselves, right on our school's campus.

Becky Schnekser, elementary
science teacher
@schnekser

Below are a few favorite games that engage students in academic review. In my classroom, I usually play these games before I assess students or to motivate students to study or review content on their own, but there's no one-size-fits-all for when to play these games. Sometimes, I use them to get kids up and out of their seats.

Classmate Search

Classmate Search can be used for any subject. Begin by handing each student a question board attached to a clipboard. The question board consists of twenty-four rectangles, and inside each rectangle, write a word or a statement. For example, if I were reviewing the state capitals with my students, each rectangle would contain the name of a state.

Additionally, each student receives a headband and a 4x6 index card folded in half. In this example, on the front of each index card would be the name of a capital city. Students place the headband around their head and insert the back half of the index card between the headband and their forehead (making sure the writing is visible to their classmates).

The game starts with students standing up and walking around the classroom. Students search for a classmate who is wearing the name of the capital for one of the states from their question board. Rather than writing the answer on the question sheet, students write the name of the classmate who is wearing the answer on their forehead. Students may not speak to each other and must keep moving around the classroom.

When the game ends, students return to their seats and remove the index cards and headbands from their heads. Finally, go over the answers by yelling out the student's name who was wearing the answer, rather than the actual answer.

Materials:

1. Game board
2. Clipboards (optional)
3. Hairbands (grab these from your local dollar store)

Cost: $

Prep time: Minimal

Players: Every student for themselves

TIP: DIFFERENTIATION

Create different game boards with fewer questions on each and print them on different-color paper. Each game board can be differentiated for the different learners in your class without them knowing it. Tell students that if they have a green game board, they are only searching for classmates wearing green headbands. If they have a yellow gameboard, they are only searching for classmates wearing yellow headbands, and so on. This is particularly helpful during math, when some students need reinforcement while other students are ready for enrichment.

Puzzlemania

I have been playing Puzzlemania for at least a decade, and you might have already seen variations of it. Take an 11x17 piece of copy paper and use a pencil to divide it up into twenty-four rectangles (six columns and four rows). Then, write different words on either side of the pencil line. The words on the corresponding sides must have a connection: they may be synonyms, antonyms, typical references, a math equation/answer, or a date and an event.

For example, one edge may say "3x2," and the corresponding side from another piece says "6." After you finish writing on all the sides, photocopy the number of puzzles you need. Then cut out each puzzle piece (along the pencil lines used to create the rectangles) and seal the pieces in a Ziploc bag. This game can be used to review almost any of the standards in

your curriculum. I most frequently use it for math, social studies, science, and vocabulary, but I've seen art teachers play this game with artists and their work and music teachers with notes, lyrics, and composers. I could imagine a PE teacher using this game as a team-building activity, having students match sports with teams or players.

beach	sand		slow	fast		ice	cream		rain	sunshine
Kevin		snow		math		square root 25				California
Butler		winter		numbers		5				Sacramento
palm	tree		rain	coat		dog	cat		apple	fruit
50		happy		money		school				fish
10 × 5		des		cash		teacher				pole
salad	dressing	8 squared	8 × 8		20 / 4	5		pizza	pie	
morning		library		television		dance				3 squared
night		books		show		party				6
secret	lie	books	pages		computer	screen		Apple	Samsung	

Group students into teams of two or three. After you give directions and show an example of a finished puzzle, each group gets a bag and must put the puzzle together by matching up the sides. When students think they have finished, check their work to make sure they made the correct matches. Warning: this game is a lot more challenging than it appears, because students learn that communicating with one another, i.e., listening to each other, is just as important as the academic content the puzzle is reviewing.

Materials:

1. Game pieces

Cost: Free!
Prep time: Minimal
Players: Pairs or small groups

TIP: DIFFERENTIATION

For students who may need additional help with completing a game like this, send them home with the game content the night before the classroom experience. For example, if you are reviewing vocabulary, send the students home with the exact words and definitions that will appear on the game as a study guide. Also, create an alternative game board with fewer pieces. Rather than twenty-four pieces, make it sixteen or twenty pieces.

Bucket Ball Bounce

I use this game primarily to review vocabulary, but it can be used in any subject. Students play this game just days before their vocabulary midterm exam, after they've spent two weeks studying their vocabulary words, in small teams of four to five players.

Before beginning, each player gets a number. For example, if there are six players per team, they would be numbered one through six, with all the ones playing against each other, the twos versus twos, and so on. The teams sit in lines next to each other and are separated by plastic tablecloths hung from the ceiling. One by one, a definition, typical reference, antonym, or synonym for one of their eighty words pops up on the classroom screen. Each team takes a turn having one of their teammates sit in the "hot seat." All the players who are not in the "hot seat" are seated on the sides of the classroom, usually just sitting on the tops of desks, in chairs, or on the floor.

Only the player who is sitting in the hot seat may answer the question. Each player gets fifteen seconds to come up with the correct answer and write it on their whiteboard. When time is up, the player holds up their whiteboard.

Every player who answers the question correctly grabs a tennis ball. Then, they must bounce their tennis ball into their team's five-gallon bucket. Each tennis ball that lands in their team's bucket earns the team a point. After each player makes their move, they trade spaces with the new player. While bouncing a tennis ball into a bucket may sound easy, it isn't.

Materials:

1. Several five-gallon buckets (from a home improvement store; clean garbage cans work, too)
2. Several dozen tennis balls
3. Content questions

Cost: $

Prep time: Minimal

Players: Teams

TIPS:

- **Shake up teams.** Divide teams into different numbers of players. For example, in a class of twenty-four students, have five teams: one team of six players, two teams of five players, and two teams of four players. This will ensure that the same students aren't always playing against one another.

- **Take notes.** I usually allow students to take notes during this activity. Since the game is usually played before an assessment, I explain to students that any question that appears in the game will most likely be on their assessment. This is a great way to keep kids who are not in the "hot seat" engaged.

- **Finding materials.** You can ask for donations of used tennis balls from parents, a local gym, the YMCA, or a nearby tennis club.

What Doesn't Belong?

This is a fun and thought-provoking activity! Place four photos of similar objects on the board. At first glance, one of the four photos doesn't seem to belong. Challenge students to make arguments for why each item does/doesn't belong with the others. For example, in math you could put up the numbers 12, 2, 23, and 44. Most students will argue that 44 doesn't fit because it doesn't have a 2 in it, but others may argue it's the 2, because it's the only single-digit number. Others might point out that 23 is the only odd number. This game can go on and on. I use this in social studies a lot, too. I will put up different historical figures or documents, and students try to argue which one doesn't belong and why.

Materials:

1. Pictures or illustrations
2. Display screen

Cost: Free

Prep time: Minimal

Players: Every student for themselves

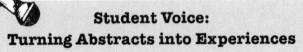

Student Voice: Turning Abstracts into Experiences

Thinking back to fifth grade, it's almost impossible to pick a favorite lesson of Mr. Butler's, but one that stands out is Fraction Foosball. The Super Bowl was coming up, and my classmates and I were excited and talking about it incessantly. So, instead of having our math class learn fractions and memorize how they function, Mr. Butler turned his classroom into a mini foosball field, and we used foosball as a means of understanding fractions. What is a complicated math subject quickly became easy and fun to learn. We understood the concepts faster because the lesson was vivid and fun and was put into terms that we as students could fully comprehend and even enjoy. Instead of struggling in math, a subject I'm not strong at, Mr. Butler's teaching allowed me to excel, because the numbers and the concepts turned into experiences I could enjoy.

Davis, class of 2016

Balloon Math

Balloon math isn't necessarily a game, but the kids love this activity when I am teaching or reviewing a less-exciting topic, like using an algorithm for solving a math problem. The way it works is simple: Print out or post the math equations on the board. Before class, inflate white latex balloons with helium (you don't need to use helium, but it really adds an extra layer of excitement and difficulty).

Students each receive one helium balloon and an assortment of permanent makers. The task is to solve each math problem using a different color marker on their balloon. Their goal? To solve all the math problems without popping the balloon or letting it float to the ceiling. This makes such a boring task (like solving double-digit multiplication) very intense.

If students pop the balloon, they continue doing the work in their notebook or on a worksheet. If students successfully keep the balloon from popping or floating to the ceiling, they get to pop the balloon at the end of the lesson. Inside the balloon, I place little slips of paper. Some students win bonus house points or a homework pass. Students know that they may only "win" what appears in the balloon if they are able to complete the entire task without popping the balloon. This helps kids work very carefully. Others simply get a fun message and congratulations for completing the task. Again, you don't need to use this game only for math. It can easily be used to achieve fluency in language arts, social studies, or science skills, too.

Materials:

1. White latex balloons
2. Sharpie markers (blunt-tipped)

Cost: $$ Sharpie markers can be expensive, but in my experience, they are the only markers that don't smudge..

Rather than buying, see if you can borrow from other teachers.

Prep time: 30 minutes (to blow up balloons)

Players: Every student for themselves

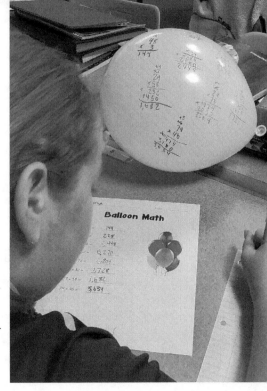

TIPS:

- **Differentiation.** Students can be given different and individualized problems to solve.

- **Heads-up.** Let your school office and classrooms nearby know there will be balloons popping in your classroom.

Tower of Answers

Students get about thirty minutes to complete as many task cards as possible. This time can be adjusted to the needs of your students or the time you have with them. Toward the end of the class period, we go over the answers to the questions. For every question students answer correctly, they get to use the task card to build a tower. I give students three or four minutes to try to build the tallest tower. The student who builds the tallest tower wins! I like this because, while it's an advantage to have more correct answers, having the most cards doesn't necessarily mean you win the tower-building contest. I also think older kids, especially middle schoolers, would love this type of challenge due to the addition of friendly competition.

Materials:

1. Task cards (preferably printed on card stock)

Cost: Free

Prep time: Minimal

Players: Independent, pairs, or small groups

TIP: DIFFERENTIATION

Not all students need to solve the same set of task cards. Task cards for different levels can be purchased from Teachers Pay Teachers.

Cube Challenge

Print out a dozen or so cube templates on paper and write different words (or numbers if doing this for math) on each cube's face. I usually use eight cubes (so the sentences must contain exactly eight words) with six different sentences or math equations. After writing all the words/numbers on the faces of the paper cubes, photocopy multiple copies of the originals. Then, assemble each of the cubes into its three-dimensional shape. Students work independently, in cooperative pairs, or in groups and must create sentences using the words written on the faces of the cubes. It's like a three-dimensional unscrambling game.

Materials:

1. Paper cube

Cost: Free

Prep time: 30 minutes

Players: Independent, pairs, or small groups

CUBE GAME EXAMPLES

George Washington was the first president of the United States.

Seven times twelve creates a product of eighty-four.

As one example, I may put a photo of someone we have been studying up on the board. Students get sixty seconds to manipulate the different cubes to create a statement about that person. Or I might put a vocabulary word up on the board, and students must use the words on the cube to come up with the definition.

Spin It!

This game is so simple! It can be used across disciplines and requires very little prep. It's especially useful when reviewing vocabulary: just give students a worksheet with the definitions of the weekly vocabulary words on them and a line next to each word for students to fill in the vocabulary word.

Students work with whomever they are sitting closest to. Each pair of students receives a game spinner with several colored sections (red, blue, yellow, purple, green). When the game begins, student A spins the spinner until they land on the color green. While student A is spinning, student B tries to write down as many vocabulary words as possible. When the spinner lands on green, student A and student B switch roles.

When the game is over (this usually takes around three to five minutes or so), the student who correctly defined the most vocabulary words is the winner. This game can also be used when studying states and capitals, reviewing basic math facts, and naming elements on the periodic table.

Materials:

1. Spinner (with different-colored sections)

Cost: $ or free (if you have or can borrow spinners)
Prep time: Minimal
Players: Cooperative pairs

TIP: DIFFERENTIATION

For some students, presenting them with an entire worksheet may be overwhelming. I sometimes cut the number of questions for students in half so it's more manageable.

Four in a Row 2.Ø

This is a simple game that turns completing a worksheet into a (friendly) competition. Print out a game board that has twenty-five circles on it set up in an array of 5x5. Each circle is numbered one through twenty-five. Students work in pairs and use a colored pencil or crayon (each a different color). Students are then given a separate worksheet (with twenty-five questions on it). Player one chooses any question from the worksheet to answer. If they answer correctly, they color in the circle that corresponds with the number of the problem they just answered. Then player two chooses a worksheet question and tries to answer it correctly so they can fill the corresponding number circle with their color. The goal is to try to color in four circles in a row. Once accomplished, students start over until all the questions are answered or time is up.

Materials:

1. Teacher-made game board
2. Crayons, colored pencils, or markers in at least two different colors

Cost: Free
Prep time: Minimal to none
Players: Cooperative pairs

TIP: DIFFERENTIATION

Not all the worksheets need to be the same. Group students with the same needs together and supply students with worksheets that meet their levels.

Human Foosball

This game can be used to review any material for any subject. Use duct tape to create a foosball-style field on the floor, then mark spots where each student will sit during the game (unlike real foosball, players cannot move). I place three players on the first line, two on the second, and one as the goalie. Students play in rounds with two teams of six competing. Alternate teams every five or six questions. Depending on the number of questions, the game usually lasts for about thirty minutes.

1. Simply create questions you want students to answer on a slideshow, such as PowerPoint or Google Slides.
2. Explain to your players that, like real foosball, the ball must remain on the ground. The ball cannot be thrown or go airborne. Any balls thrown into the goal do not count.
3. Assign students places to sit on the field and remind them they are to stay seated throughout the game. I do this by placing masking tape Xs on the floor.

4. Give each student a whiteboard and a dry-erase marker. Paper and markers will work, too.

5. Reveal a question on the board. Give students ample time to answer/solve the question on their whiteboard.

6. When the time is up, ask students to hold up their answers. The number of students who answer correctly equals the amount of time students get to "play" foosball. For example, if ten players answer correctly, students get ten seconds of playing time by trying to roll the ball into their goal.

7. Every goal made is equal to a point.

8. Students who are not playing also answer questions, but their correct answers do not count toward earned playing time.

9. Repeat until all questions are answered and all students have had a chance to play.

Materials:

1. Duct tape (ideally red and blue)
2. Pinnies, optional (ideally red and blue)
3. Medium-sized foam ball

4. 2 small nets or 4 cones to be used as the goal

Cost: $$

Prep time: 45–60 minutes

Players: 6 vs. 6, in rounds

TIP:

If possible, borrow pinnies from the PE department. You can also assign students colors beforehand and ask them to wear that color to school. Plastic leis from a party store are also a fun and low-cost way to differentiate teams.

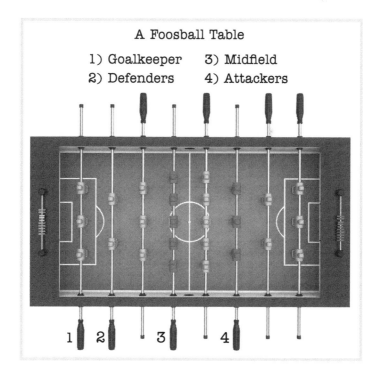

A Foosball Table

1) Goalkeeper 3) Midfield
2) Defenders 4) Attackers

Educator Spotlight:
Progress over Perfection

Coming to education as a second career from warehousing and logistics, progress was not my initial goal. I blindly demanded perfection and justified my relentless push as "maintaining high expectations." I quickly realized, however, that progress over perfection should be the approach, as we are working with human beings. All from different backgrounds, at different levels, with different abilities, and developing at different rates.

This epiphany helped shape my outlook and my teaching toward a more patient and gracious concept, even given today's bottom-line focus on state testing scores (another soapbox entirely). How many students in our classrooms arrive at the correct answer each and every time, without encountering stumbling blocks, incorrect thinking, or failure?

On the first day of school, I introduce challenges such as Cookie Face (a "minute-to-win-it" game where you place a cookie on your forehead, then manipulate and move it to your mouth without using your hands) to create a safe environment for learning, perseverance, and low-stakes failure. My hope is that this will lay the foundation for students to draw upon those skills in a greater capacity when necessary.

Teaching is the practice of instructing, observing, redirecting,

cajoling, and celebrating (not necessarily in that order), with the payoff being a front-row seat to witness that magical "lightbulb" moment when a student grasps something through constant progress, rather than immediate perfection.

David Domena, elementary teacher
@mrdelemntary

ACTION!

1. How have you used games to review content and engage students in active learning?

2. Identify three ways to ensure all students are active participants in classroom games.

3. Are you able to adapt one of the games mentioned above into the content you're teaching in your classroom? If so, how?

CHAPTER THREE

Field of Dreams

Classroom Culture

*I*f *you build it, [they] will come.* That is the famous line from the
1989 baseball movie *Field of Dreams.* Iowa farmer Ray (Kevin
Costner) hears a voice one night telling him, "If you build it, he will
come," prompting him to build a baseball diamond on his cornfield in
hope of luring the ghosts of great baseball players to his field. As teachers taking the time to build our classroom, culture matters. Getting
to know our students as individuals not only helps us, as educators,
build relationships but aids student development. Forming authentic
relationships with our students sets the climate for the classroom—a
positive classroom flourishes when students perceive that we care
about them.

In my experience, the classroom climate is a perception-based
vision, while the culture is about shared values and beliefs. Broadly
speaking, climate is how people feel in your classroom, and culture is a
deeper aspect of how people behave in your classroom.

> **Classroom Climate vs. Classroom Culture**
>
> Climate is a perception-based vision, while culture consists of shared values and beliefs.
> **Climate** – How people feel in your classroom
> **Culture** – How people behave in your classroom

Without a sense of strong classroom climate, it will be challenging to build classroom culture. I will again use a houseplant comparison. Houseplants won't flourish if they aren't provided with the right conditions. The correct amount of light, water, humidity. When I give my houseplants the right climate, the plants thrive. This is the same in the classroom. I can't just love them; I need to take action. Teachers are responsible for creating an environment where our students have the chance to thrive.

I'm often asked how some teachers have students who struggled in previous grades begin to flourish in their classes. While there is no one answer, I think one of the main ingredients is the strong bonds some teachers are able build with their students. In my own experience as a teacher, I genuinely believe that if the majority of our students enjoy us, trust us, feel safe, and—crucially—respect us, the academics fall into place. Personally, I would never be able to get students to reach the high academic goals I set for them without creating strong relationships with them. I believe relationships come first, then everything else.

Quick Tips for Building Positive Classroom Culture

- Normalize that people make mistakes, including yourself.
- Complete challenging tasks with students, rather than just assigning them. Show them the struggle.
- Model and showcase excellent work by showing students examples of what you expect.

- Share stories of your own time in school, both the successes and failures you experienced.
- Emphasize effort over grades.

The Mood Meter

An awareness of mood and mindset is important when building classroom culture. In my classroom, students use a Mood Meter each morning to identify and acknowledge how they are feeling and what they can do to set goals for the day. Developed by the Yale Center for Emotional Intelligence, this tool sets students up for success by helping them manage their emotions. The center's website describes it as follows:

> The Mood Meter is one of the "anchors of Emotional Intelligence" in Yale's RULER program. It helps people develop the core RULER skills: Recognizing, Understanding, Labeling, Expressing, and Regulating emotions.
>
> The Mood Meter develops emotional intelligence over time. Learning to identify and label emotions is a critical step toward cultivating emotional intelligence. Using the Mood Meter can help you become more mindful of how your emotions change throughout the day and how your emotions in turn affect your actions. Using the Mood Meter can help you to develop self-awareness and self-regulation, it's important to understand the full scope of your emotional life.

On the first day of school, I provide every student with a Mood Meter, which I've printed on half-page labels so students can stick them into their morning journals. There's now a Mood Meter app that can be downloaded for students and for schools that have 1:1 devices or a bring-your-own-device program.

In Kim Bearden's book *Fight Song*, she writes about the importance of mindset both in your daily life and in the classroom. During times of high stress (and we've all had a few of those lately), it's easy to have a negative mindset. However, Kim discusses how we have the power to modify our mindset and notes the difference this can make in our overall well-being. By teaching students about negative and modified mindsets, we allow them to develop sufficient confidence to own and accept their feelings, which gives them the agency to do something about issues they're facing. Recognizing mindsets can come from writing about their feeling in a journal, talking to a teacher or friend, or seeking out help from a school counselor.

Ideas to Promote Student Communication for SEL:

1. Set up a "mailbox" on or near your desk where students can place notes for you.
2. Provide exit slips at the end of the day/class period where they can write down questions.
3. Poll students using Google Forms.
4. Set up office hours, a dedicated time when students can meet with you one-on-one or in a small group.

As educators, we know how perceptive our students are. While for a moment they may enjoy a teacher who shows movies, gives extra recess, or allows them to have free time, there's no relationship-building in those activities. Twenty years later, no one looks back and says the teacher who sat at their desk and showed a movie or allowed them to have recess all day made a difference in their lives. Kids will recall the teachers who made a difference. The ones who pushed them outside of their comfort zone, who took the time to make memories and build bonds with them.

Teaching in New York, we awaited the replacement of the long, cold of winter with spring. When spring finally arrived, on that first warm day I would take my students outside and play kickball games with them. Students knew, however, that to earn that extra fifteen or twenty minutes, they would need to work twice as hard, but they still loved that I played with them. We were all vested in a common goal of having fun. Yes, it's okay to have fun with your students, but I believe there is a fine line between fun and too much fun.

A few years ago, I was fortunate enough to have a student tell me that I know the exact combination of making school fun, being strict, and teaching kids everything they need to know. I laughed and asked her to explain. She told me she'd once had a teacher who just wanted to joke all day and have fun. While this student admitted that school had been easy, she said she never actually *learned* anything. She said she'd also had teachers who only wanted to teach all day and never have fun, which eventually made school boring.

How do we as educators walk this fine line? I think it all goes back to the time we take to build the relationships we have with our students. In my classroom, students know I am foremost their teacher, a figure of authority—but they also know I care about them and consider myself their friend. In nineteen years in the classroom, I've never yelled at a student (not to say I haven't wanted to, but we all have those days). Usually, all I need to do is put a slight change in the tone of my voice or raise an eyebrow, or ask to speak to them privately.

I'm known for running a tight ship, but my classroom is by no means a dictatorship. From the first day of school, I tell students that this is *our* classroom and also make them aware of the high standards I will hold them to and that I don't accept excuses. I spend a lot of time teaching them to be proactive and to self-advocate for themselves. They know I am there to help them and do whatever it takes to get them where they need to go. As tough as I am, I'm also fair. "One-size-fits-all" does not work in any facet of education. While there are rules and expectations for everyone to follow, there are also exceptions to the rules. Teachers cannot expect every student to fit a mold. Every child is different, just as every home is different. These differences are why it's vital to get to know each child both as a student and as a person.

Creating the Culture Rules:

1. Involve all students in the process.
2. Avoid the "do nots." Begin with "do."
3. Create the rules together as a class and try giving them a unique name, such as Our Classroom Bill of Rights.
4. Have students vote on which rules to include. Revise and edit as needed.
5. Supply students with a personal copy of the rules as a reference as well as displaying the rules in the classroom.

Much of what I do to build bonds with my students is rather simple. I'm a big believer that teachers should begin the day (or class period) on a strong note. For example, standing outside the classroom door every morning to greet my students with a verbal "good morning" and a high five or fist pump. When students walk into the classroom, music is playing and we use the first few minutes of class to settle in, catch up with a friend, and get workspaces organized.

Also, we as teachers should eat lunch with our students. Not every day, but once a week or as your schedule allows. It's a major game changer. I do my best to have lunch or a snack with my students twice a week. It's illuminating to see them in social settings and to keep up with what interests them. Just sitting and observing the different social groups that form during lunch can be both fascinating and telling. Sometimes the most challenging student in your academic class is the student you want to sit next to the most at lunch.

Once a trimester, I host a "Golden Lunch," by invite only. Using handwritten invitations, I invite approximately one-third of the class to have a special lunch with me. I borrow a long folding table and set it with a gold tablecloth, gold plates, gold plasticware, and gold cups I've purchased from the dollar store. The purpose is to celebrate students who have been working toward reaching their goals. These goals may be academic, personal, or social. Some students are invited to several Golden Lunches over the course of the year; other students may not get invited at all. It varies from year to year, depending on the group of students I have.

Another thing I've realized is the power of authentic feedback. We've all visited classrooms where, after a student gives a presentation or shares a project, all the teacher does is give positive feedback and tell the student how wonderful the presentation was. While we may all like compliments, it's essential that we give meaningful feedback along with positive comments. Genuine, constructive feedback is respectful of students' time, and helps us become better educators.

Ideas for giving constructive feedback:

- Begin with a strength or compliment.
- Pinpoint a specific area where a student can grow, along with an action they can use to improve.
- Ask the student what questions you can answer for them or how you can help them.
- Include peers in the constructive feedback forum.

Students also able to provide me with feedback. As scary as that sounds, I give students several opportunities to give me feedback and share suggestions on how to make our class better. On Fridays, I hold class meetings where students can share how their week went and give shout-outs to their classmates. In addition, I do monthly feedback forms using Google Forms, where students can submit their own comments and questions about things that occurred during class. As a teacher, I've received insightful feedback from my students, like some students being unable to see the board in the afternoon because of the glare from the sun. Once I knew about it, I was able to simply place a piece of posterboard over the window, and the problem was solved.

Recently, I've also added a mailbox to the side of my desk. Not for mail, but as a place where students can drop in notes saying anything they want. Notes can be anonymous or can include their names. It's a great tool for students who may not be comfortable with self-advocating orally in front of others, or at all. Students must know that their ideas, thoughts, and opinions matter, and this is a clear way to communicate that to them.

My students also know I love my job. I tell them about how, when I was their age, all I wanted to do was become a teacher. I joke with them that I've been in fifth grade for eighteen years, and maybe one day I will make it to sixth grade. They know that because of them, I have the best job in the world!

The Morning Co-Host Show

We as teachers can do so much more with kids when they trust us. One of the tools I use to engender trust and gain knowledge of students is morning meetings. And morning meetings aren't just for primary students: some of the best morning meetings (aka "class meetings") I have seen have taken place in middle and high school classrooms. While the format of my own morning meetings has changed over the years, the concept has stayed the same. It's a sacred time to begin each day together as a classroom community.

Each of my students has a morning journal. Each day, when students enter my classroom, the first thing they do is take out their journals and answer two questions written on the board. The first question is always the same: "How are you feeling today, and why?" Students use the Mood Meter to gauge their feelings and then take a minute to connect those feelings to their possible causes (knowing that sometimes there isn't one). The second question varies from "Would you rather eat pizza for a year or live without electricity for a month?" and "If you had $1,000 to give away, who would you give it to, and why?"

Morning Journal Question Ideas

- What's your very first memory?
- What's your favorite board game?
- Would you rather watch a sad or scary movie?
- If you could be any animal for a day, what would you be?
- What's your favorite holiday?
- Would you rather be able to fly or read people's minds?
- If you could be a character in any book, who would you be?
- Would you rather switch places with your teacher or parents for a day?
- What is one thing most people don't know about you?
- Would you rather set the table before dinner or clean up the table after dinner?
- Would you rather live in the mountains or at the beach?
- What is something that brings you joy?
- Would you rather be four feet tall for the rest of your life or eight feet tall for the rest of your life?
- If you had a car, what color would it be and why?
- Would you rather receive flowers or chocolates as a gift?
- If you received $1,000 to give away, who would you give it to?
- What's your favorite day of the week?

- Would you rather be able to move things with your mind or have supersonic hearing?
- If you could spend the day with anyone, living or dead, who would it be?

After the two questions, our Morning Co-Host Show begins. Each day, a different student becomes my co-host and helps run our morning meeting, which lasts about fifteen minutes. The co-host gets to practice their presentation and leadership skills. If you mixed the beginning of *Live with Kelly and Ryan* with the games that Jimmy Fallon plays on *The Tonight Show*, you would end up with our Morning Co-Host Show.

Student Voice:
Morning Co-Host Show

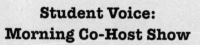

I really remember having co-hosts and how exciting it would be to be picked. We became a celebrity for fifteen minutes, and the student(s) were in charge of the interactions of our morning meeting. When I wasn't the co-host, it was always fun to see what my friends would do as co-host.

I think writing in a journal every day was a good opportunity to reflect on things that were happening and ask myself questions. Also, at the beginning of the year, Mr. Butler sat me down and explained to me that sometimes I acted like I knew it all. This feedback was really important to me, and I'm very thankful for him, because after that I learned to listen to others rather than always yelling out my answers. My mom thanked him, too.

Max, class of 2020

During the first few minutes of *Live*, Kelly Ripa and Ryan Seacrest chat about their lives, things happening globally, and positive news stories. My co-host and I begin by talking about what we did the previous night after school. I may talk about where I had dinner or something I watched on television, while my students may share about their sports practices or dance lessons. One of us shares a current event or crazy news story from the day before. After that, we each share our responses to the question of the day.

The co-host will then choose students (at random) to share their journal responses. After seven or eight students have shared, the co-host and I will usually play a game, often inspired by the games Jimmy Fallon plays with his guests on *The Tonight Show*. It may be a round of Name that Tune, a Minute-to-Win-It match, Lies in a Box, or even the Limbo. We've become so good at our morning shows that I think we could sell tickets and have a live audience. Kids love being the co-host, and this is probably my favorite ten to fifteen minutes of the school day. Relationships matter.

Morning Show Rundown

1. Students sign up in advance to be the morning co-host by writing their name on a paper calendar.
2. The teacher and co-host share what they did after school.
3. The co-host or teacher shares a current event, newsworthy topic, or school happening.
4. The co-host and teacher answer the question of the day.
5. The co-host picks a handful of students to share their answers from the question of the day.
6. The co-host and teacher (or on occasion the entire class) play a quick game.
7. The meeting ends with the day's weather, a joke, or a teaser about what to expect the next day.

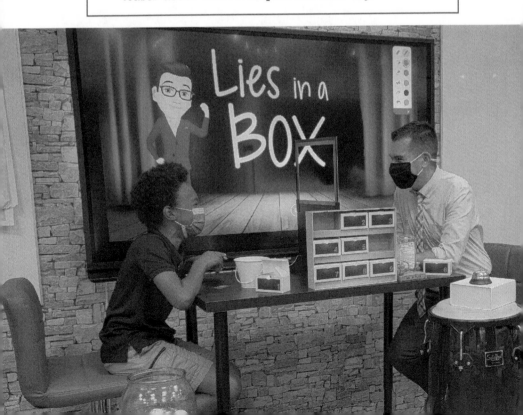

Reading Aloud

Reading aloud is a powerful relationship-builder, too. If there were one thing I'd recommend teachers do every day, it is to read aloud to your class for pleasure. The research substantiating the many beneficial effects of reading aloud to children is incontrovertible. Reading to kids for pleasure is not only magical and community-building, it is also the perfect way to integrate social justice, SEL, and diversity lessons.

Reading every day to my kids is a nonnegotiable. In my opinion, it's simply the easiest way to build community. We read a different picture book (pictures books aren't just for primary classrooms), and if I somehow forget, my students will quickly call me out. Sometimes we read funny books, sometimes serious books, and sometimes I read them books connected to the content we are learning about. And if it's a day with a lot going on, we'll read part of a book and continue it the next day. We also read a variety of full-length novels that may take several weeks to finish reading together. There's something magical that occurs in this shared experience between teachers and students.

One of my students' favorite things about our daily read-alouds is what I call "alternate endings," which have become a little classroom ritual after we finish a book. I don't do this with every book we read, but I tell students that sometimes authors will send me "special" copies of books that have an "alternative" ending. Kids LOVE this. I will reread the last page or two and then add a ridiculous ending. So simple, but so fun.

Also, I tell my favorite story to students each Halloween. First, I buy a few black plastic tablecloths from the party store and hang them from the ceiling to turn a corner of my classroom into a haunted room. Then, I hang up some spooky decorations and turn on some blacklights. Students are invited into "the haunted corner" to listen to a spooky story. The spooky story is about them! Throughout the harrowing tale, every student has a cameo appearance. (Spoiler: I use the same story every year but swap out the names.) The kids love it, and it's just suspenseful enough to keep them on the edge of their seats.

If nothing else, get to know your students. Students want to feel seen and heard. I am always giving students an outlet to express their thoughts, whether in a formal setting during a lesson or during our class meeting times. They want to feel connected with their teacher and when that connection is made, the rewards are endless.

My Top 20 Favorite Picture Books

- *What Do Teachers Do (after YOU Leave School)?*
- *The Circles All Around Us*
- *Llama Destroys the World*
- *Ada's Violin*
- *The Serious Goose*
- *Raise Your Hand*
- *The 5 O'Clock Band*
- *Woosh!*
- *Mr. Peabody's Apples*
- *Albert*
- *Last Stop on Market Street*
- *Mr. Ferris and His Wheel*
- *The Scarlet Stocking Spy*
- *Does It Fart?*
- *Fry Bread*
- *Freedom on the Menu*
- *The Name Jar*
- *Malala's Magical Pencil*
- *Ribbit!*
- *Enemy Pie*

A few years ago, there was a student in my class whom I just wasn't able to connect with. She seemed nervous and uncomfortable, no matter how much guidance I gave her. I played the good guy and the bad guy and everything in between, but nothing was working. I reached out to her former teachers, who gave me some guidance. Her third grade teacher told me part of connecting with this particular student was not only to have clear expectations, but to share a love for the LA Dodgers.

I snuck a look into this student's locker and yup, it was covered with LA Dodger memorabilia. Stickers, magnets, a baseball, everything you can imagine a ten-year-old fitting in their locker. So, the next day, I did what I needed to do. I hung up a small souvenir pennant above my desk, made sure I carefully watched the game on television the night before, and the next day, I wore a Dodger shirt to school. When she walked up the stairs, my first words to her were, "Wow, did you see the Dodgers game?" After that, the student's behavior became more positive, and she wrote me a very kind letter of appreciation. This student and I built a mutual trust and understanding with each other. Now, I wish everything were as easy as that, but sometimes it is, and when it is, it makes life so much simpler.

It's Okay to Laugh Together

Sometimes as teachers we can forget it's okay to laugh. Some of my fondest moments of teaching have been when the class and I erupted into uncontrollable laughter. Laughing is a human quality and shows students that we teachers are humans, too. A few years ago, during a lesson on how to conduct internet research, one of my best-behaved and diligent workers asked if she could google me. Before I could say no, the class had already put my name into the Google search bar and hit "search."

I don't recommend having your students google you, because you cannot control the things other people with your name have done! However, in this situation, it was too late to stop them. They searched for images of Kevin Butler and found the results (none which were actually me) extremely amusing. Upon looking at their computer screens, I laughed, too. It was a funny few minutes. And it actually added to the lesson afterward: there's a *lot* of misinformation on the internet.

Educator Spotlight:
Relationship-Building

Building relationships with students is the most important thing in my second grade classroom. I always tell parents on Back to School Night that the academics will come, but my job is to help students leave as better people. Learning how to respect one another, work with others, and solve problems is something I try to embed in our classroom culture, as well as helping students create relationships with each other and with me. One way that I try to foster and maintain relationships is to bring things they love and relate to into the classroom. For example, this school year, my students LOVE sports. From gymnastics, to football, to baseball, to basketball, almost every single one of my students loves to play, talk, or read about sports.

This winter was the 2022 Beijing Winter Olympics. Knowing that my students love and appreciate sports, I decided to plan and create a week where our classroom would turn into an Olympic village, and students would be able to participate in various Olympics-themed learning activities. From researching Olympic sports, to competing in Olympic math events, to building their own bobsleds out of STEM materials, students were not only engaged but also so excited to be a part of our classroom.

Students completed standards-based activities in different and engaging ways, such as using iPads to research a sport and then write multiparagraph essays about that sport. They used the Book Creator app to create a virtual book about Beijing. They used toilet paper rolls, straws, and tape to made bobsleds that could successfully slide down our playground's twisty slide.

Knowing what your students love and bringing that into the classroom is an instant way to add magic to their learning.

Whitney Ramirez,
first and second grade teacher
@learningwithcrayons

ACTION!

1. List three ways you form relationships with your students in the classroom.

2. Describe the classroom rituals or routines that help build community in your classroom.

3. How would your students describe the climate of your classroom?

4. How would your students describe you: too fun, too strict, or just right?

5. In what ways do you keep a balance between praise and giving constructive feedback to your students?

6. Do you read to your class for pleasure? If not, is there a way to fit it into your routine?

CHAPTER FOUR

Akeelah and the Bee

Relationships Matter

A keelah and the Bee is the story of an eleven-year-old girl who lives in Los Angeles and discovers she has a knack for spelling, which leads her to the National Spelling Bee. While her mother at first objects, it is the love and encouragement from her teacher and coach that help her follow her dreams while also realizing there are more important things in her life than winning the championship. Relationships and people are more important.

Recently, a student from my very first class got married. How has time has gone by so quickly? I remember Ryan in my classroom as if it were yesterday. He always came to school with a positive attitude, ready to learn something new and already smarter than me. His parents were teachers, and his mom actually worked at the middle school I'd attended. His father worked at the high school of the district where I taught.

Building relationships with our students, to me, is what makes the teaching profession like no other. Every student in our classroom is different, and it's important that we as teachers don't just recognize their differences, but also take the time to get to know each individual. Students who feel respected, trusted, and held accountable by their teacher are much more likely to thrive in their classroom setting. Early in the school year, I tell my students I hold such high expectations for them because I truly believe one of my students will be the president of the United States. It's my responsibility to teach them everything I can so that when they become president, they will tell everyone about their great fifth grade teacher. Regardless of whether or not a student of mine becomes president, they deserve to be treated as if their lives and their decisions are important. Because they are.

On the last day of school, I tell students, "Once a student of mine, always a student of mine." For the last twelve years, I have attended all of my former fifth graders' high school graduation ceremonies. The past year was the last group of kids I taught in New York to graduate from high school. After flying from Los Angeles to New York, I learned that due to Covid-19 restrictions, I would be unable to attend the actual ceremony (rules and guidelines were changing by the hour at that time). So in lieu of seeing them, I quickly messaged several of the parents of these former fifth graders and asked them to spread the word that I would love to see the kids while I was in New York. Within hours, former students were texting me! We decided that after

their graduation rehearsal, we would meet at a diner for lunch. These students said they'd find all their former classmates and make sure everyone was invited.

It was a beautiful June day, 80 degrees and sunny. After I arrived at the diner, I became a little nervous that I would be the only person sitting at a table for twenty-four. What if these students were just too busy right now, with prom and dates and family? This group of kids were extra special to me because they were the last. I loved this class. I remember clear as day when I stood up on the desk and shared with them that I was moving to California. There was a lot of crying.

But one by one over the next fifteen minutes, my former fifth graders trickled into the diner: some alone, others in pairs. Nick was the first to arrive. Not only was I happy to see him, I was also relieved I wouldn't be sitting at the table on my own after all! He walked in with a huge smile on his face, and all I could think was, *This is my why.* So here we were, a reunion seven years in the making. It was great seeing them and talking to each of them, and after a few minutes, I just sat back and took it all in. Twenty or so seventeen- and eighteen-year-olds. For most, this was the first time they had been in the same room together in years. As we all do, they had gravitated to new friends and new interests. Some had even moved away, but here we were again, all together.

As they reminisced about everything from our house system to songs I had sung and games we had played, I couldn't believe how much they remembered. Listening to them share what their plans were for after high school brought me such happiness. Most were headed off to college, others to vocational school, and one or two were undecided.

A few students even requested that I FaceTime with their parents. When building relationships with students, we are also building relationships with their families. It was pretty cool that so many of the parents were as excited to see me as my students were. Even years later, when I head back home, I still visit the families of former students.

As I said, this lunch reminded me of my own why. After more than a year of teaching during a pandemic, mostly on Zoom, I wasn't sure if I could continue doing this job. Teaching virtually was not fun. This lunch—these kids—rekindled my passion for teaching. Relationships matter.

Building relationships with your students is a vital ingredient in directing a successful classroom climate. I'm sometimes shocked by the end-of-year forms teachers fill out to pass on to the next year's teacher. and how little they know about their students! I recommend prioritizing that relationship from day one. During back-to-school presentations, I thank parents for trusting me with their children. I open by mentioning that I probably spend more time with their children during the weekdays than they do, and I certainly spend more time with them than I do with my own family and friends. Two or three months later, during our first parent-teacher conference, I remind parents of those statements and begin the conference by sharing everything I have learned about their children.

An entire wall in my classroom is dedicated to family photos. Every year, I ask students to bring in one recent family photo. I enlarge these photos on a color copier, frame them with frames I buy at the dollar store, and hang them up in our classroom. It's a reminder that we are a family and a community. I've seen this idea in classrooms across the country. This picture wall is one of the first things people comment on when they come to my classroom for the first time, and it's one of the key components to creating an open, respectful climate. When kids see that you are a family, it allows the growth of positive classroom culture.

In "normal times" I have an end-of-the-year ritual. I print out a photo of each student with the word "is . . . " next to it. I attach each paper to a clipboard, and we sit in a circle. Every thirty seconds, students pass the clipboard to the person to their right. Each person writes down something about you: a memory, a positive word, or anything else that would make you feel good. At the end, every student has a piece of paper covered with positive words from their peers. We attach this to their yearbooks, and I challenge students to keep it forever. I tell them that they will have bad days, and when those days come, take that paper out and read it. Then, I usually shed a few tears, give them a speech about what a wonderful year it has been, and that "once my student, always my student" speech. Then, we walk out to the buses, and I hug each student and thank them for their hard work and dedication.

The last day of school in 2020 was a half day. I had a beautiful picture book to read and naively thought it would be the last day I would have to teach on Zoom. How do you properly say goodbye to people on Zoom? I expected I would still give my speech and then just say goodbye and hit "End." Well, that's not how it went. School was supposed to end at 11:30. At 11:00, I read my last-day read-aloud (*I Wish You More*) and then had a little soap-box speech memorized to share before letting them begin their summer vacation.

Less than fifteen seconds into the speech, I was crying. Not a few tears: I was bawling. Like, hot-mess, couldn't-talk crying. I'd had no idea how much we had bonded, especially over the last two months. These kids were pioneers in education: not only did I flip my teaching style; they flipped their learning style. We had check-ins, nightly game nights, I had gone to each of their homes to deliver them a special surprise, and we even were on *The Kelly Clarkson Show* together.

And when I looked at the screen, the kids were crying, too. Not one or two of them, but all twenty-four of them. I did my best to pull it together and get through the rest of my words of wisdom (with snot falling out of my nose), to end the meeting, and then . . . I couldn't do it. Click "End." It seemed inhuman. My entire teaching career was based around forming relationships with students, and I was going to click a button and end it all? Students begged me not to end the meeting. One by one they had their own things to say. For over an hour, we sat their crying together. I needed this; they needed this; we needed this. The last two months had been like something from a whole different type of blockbuster movie. One about endurance and connection during several months of living in a global pandemic. And here were twenty-five people sitting on Zoom, crying about how much we loved one another.

After an hour, one by one, students gradually signed off. It would be another thirty minutes or so before the last student left, and I clicked "End." There's no button to end meaningful relationships.

Storytelling: Narrative Nonfiction

Our students love listening to stories. In addition to reading fiction aloud to my students, I have worked hard to develop my lessons through the art of nonfiction storytelling. Before I begin a new unit, I'll often summarize the new material into a story, doing my best to captivate my students' attention. I try to pull each of them in, often putting their own names into the wonder of the concept we will begin learning about. In her book *Expedition Science*, Becky Schnekser does a great job explaining how she uses storytelling. As she shares stories of her own incredible journeys through the Amazon, exploring rainforests and almost being eaten by a jaguar, she uses the story to connect to the content she is teaching her young scientists.

I love teaching social studies, especially American history. When beginning one of our first units of study, students learn about a group of people who mysteriously disappeared, not leaving any clues for anyone to find. When students enter the classroom, the lights are dimmed and there's eerie music playing in the background. I tell them that there's a mystery to be a solved. The mystery of over one hundred settlers vanishing from an island, from the coast of what is now known as North Carolina. That these settlers survived a two-month journey across the Atlantic Ocean, disease, vermin, and even shark attacks, but after their leader, John White, went back to Europe to get additional supplies for the colony, he returned to nothing. What could have happened? Alien abduction?

I've now got their attention. We then use various secondary sources to gather information about who these people were and historians' theories about what may have happened to the Roanoke settlers. Students

then draw their own conclusions (supported by text evidence) and report back to the class with their findings. There in that one lesson, you can hit a dozen standards on Colonial America—because students were first gripped by a real-life mystery.

Sometimes, I also tell students stories about myself when I was a student. I will tell them the good, the bad, and the ugly so they understand that I know what it is like to be a kid. I tell them about when I was a finalist in the school's science fair in third grade when someone damaged my project during the exhibition, and how upset I was. I tell them about how in fifth grade I created an entire candy company, selling candy to my friends. That I would buy the candy at a discount store and mark up the price, but then I got caught selling it at school and had to pivot to only selling it outside of the school day. That I had terrible handwriting and my teachers made me rewrite assignments numerous times until I finally submitted quality work. These stories all help build meaningful connections that bridge the years.

Passion Projects

Halfway through the year, students do Ted Talks. They each choose a passion and must create a three-minute presentation for the class, with no notes, no notecards, no slideshow, just a memorized presentation. Students are not permitted to use props, but they are encouraged to work the stage and use their voice and hands to captivate the audience. I love this project for so many reasons:

1. I learn so much about each of them.
2. I usually learn something that I knew nothing about beforehand.
3. There's no grading. In lieu of a grade, students receive constructive feedback from their peers. They pick three people. The first will give them a compliment, the second person gives them feedback on how they can become better at public speaking, and the third asks a question about their passion. I do nothing but listen and learn.

I rarely lecture or do direct teaching for more than fifteen minutes for any given subject. Instead, students are constantly working in cooperative pairs or in small groups. This collaborative learning model requires us to spend time at the beginning of the year learning procedures and going over expectations. Because we do so much learning out of our seats, students must be taught the process of engaging in this kind of process. They learn specific expectations for what cooperative group work looks like, and we spend time

talking about what it means to collaborate and the difference between a leader and a boss.

COOPERATIVE GROUP WORK EXPECTATIONS

- All members contribute and are scored on what they contributed. This means not everyone in a group may receive the same score/grade.
- All members may voice their opinions without criticism.
- All members are expected to respect the viewpoints of their group members.
- Work should be divided equally among group members.
- Each group should appoint a point person to relay concerns to the teacher.

- All members are expected to participate in presenting their work to the class (when applicable).
- All group members should be part of revising/proofreading work.

Leader vs. Boss	
Leader	**Boss**
Helps people learn what to do	Tells people what to do
Communicates kindly	Yells
Willing to learn	May act like they know it all
Thinks of others	Cares only about themselves
Shares credit	Takes credit
Others want to follow	Makes people follow
Uses pronouns such as *we*, *us*, and *our*	Uses pronouns such as *I* and *me*
Unselfish	Selfish
Listens	Tells

I credit the Ron Clark Academy house system for adding to the culture of my classroom. After my first visit to RCA, in 2009, the house system was the first thing I implemented in my classroom. I was immediately obsessed with the idea, and it's all I could think of on my flight home from Atlanta. The next day back, I challenged my fifth graders to think of names for our houses. Like RCA, I wanted the names behind each house to mean something. Students researched words in other languages, and we came up with:

Amicus: The purple house of friendship,

Bellator: The red house of warriors,

Coragem: The green house of courage, and

Phoenix: The orange house of determination.

This is now a first day of school tradition, and it's probably one of my favorite things we do as a class. A week before I place students into their houses, I begin talking about the expectations of the house system. The kids get very excited. I purchase some color-themed decorations from the party store and ask a local apparel company to create and donate team shirts for my students. This is a huge help in making the day special.

On the day students are placed into their houses, I turn the energy level up to an all-time high. Unlike RCA, I don't have a big fancy wheel for students to spin, so students pick their houses out of a spray-painted cauldron from the party store. Magical-sounding music plays in the background and the lights are turned off. One thing I really wanted—but was told I couldn't have—was a fog machine. The custodial staff said I would set off the fire alarms. However, one at a time, students are called up to the golden cauldron, stick their hand in, and pull out a purple, red, green, or orange beaded necklace signifying what house they were now a part of. Students then run into one of the corners of the room to join the rest of their new housemates.

Throughout the year, students work with their houses to complete both academic and team-building challenges. Students can earn points for their houses for outstanding citizenship, good sportsmanship, and earning perfect scores on tests and quizzes. If a student earns a point for their house, they add the point to our class scoreboard and place their picture on the board (I keep a box of all of my students' school photos near the board, laminated with a magnet on the back). The rest of the day, the class knows that student did something to help their house earn a point. Once a point is earned, it can never be taken away. As I explain to students (and parents) at the beginning of the year, there

is no tangible prize for winning the house cup. At the end of the year, the winning house is celebrated at our end-of-the-year house banquet. During the banquet, each student (regardless of what house they are in) receives a unique award, and the students of the winning house also get a small (plastic) trophy. The entire banquet is decorated in the winning house color, and students celebrate by eating lunch together. For ideas on the house system, I recommend checking out the Ron Clark Academy's website, as they have an entire section dedicated to it.

Award Ideas

- Amazing Attitude Award
- Perseverance Award
- Creativity Award
- The Strategist Award
- The Renaissance Man/Woman Award
- Master of Technology Award

- The Gratitude Award
- The Great Growth Award
- The Goal Crusher Award
- Charisma Award

An Amazing Race

I'm a huge fan of the reality television show *The Amazing Race* and wanted to have an Amazing Race with my students. I knew this could be a perfect house challenge and team-building exercise. Students are given two weeks to review and study various vocabulary words we have learned in class. These words provide the academic tie-in to the game. During the Amazing Race, within their houses students are challenged with completing a scavenger hunt and solving three academic tasks.

Materials:

1. 8 various riddle (clue) cards (1 set for each team)
2. 10 clue envelopes (legal sized, 2 decoy)
3. Letter cards: *T, E, A, M, W, O, R, K* (8 per team, placed inside clue envelopes, printed on different colors of paper), plus two fake cards with the letters *B* and *C*.
4. Detour & Roadblock cards (2 for each team)
5. 3 Tasks (word scramble, definitions, Puzzlemania game)

Cost: $

Prep time: 60–120 minutes (first time takes longest, but I save everything, which makes the next race much easier to prep)

Players: Whole class, divided into equal-sized teams (ideally 4–5 students per team)

SCAVENGER HUNT

I create riddles which, when solved, reveal locations around our school's campus.

> **Example:** Don't be scared to add some color to your life! You might be able to find van Gogh or Picasso at this location. Find the envelope outside of this room.

At the beginning of the race, each team gets their first of eight riddles (printed on a card), which reveals the first location they must find. When teams get to the location, they look for a clue envelope and remove a card that matches their house color. A letter of the alphabet is printed on each card. Teams return to the classroom with the letter card and exchange it for their next riddle. Note: the letters of the index cards let me know if the team went to the correct location (instead of just running around the school looking for envelopes). If the team comes back with the wrong letter, they have to go back, return the index card, and try again. There are a total of eight envelopes students must find.

Letter cards. The letter cards spell out T-E-A-M-W-O-R-K. Only I know that, but it helps me keep track of whether teams return with the correct card. (I put the letters *B* and *C* on the fake cards in the "decoy" envelopes.)

Task 1: Detour. Just like the television show, students get a detour (and roadblock: see task 3). The purpose of the detour is for teams to accomplish an academic task. Since my Amazing Race is themed around vocabulary, the detour task asks students to work together as a team to unscramble the spellings of twelve of their vocabulary words. Once completed, they get their next clue and continue the race.

Task 2: Roadblock. Similar to the detour, the roadblock is another academic task. Students are given twelve definitions and must write the vocabulary word that fits each definition. Again, teams work together to complete the task, and once finished, they get the next clue and continue the race.

Task 3: Puzzlemania. After students finish the scavenger hunt, the detour, and the roadblock, their final task is a giant Puzzlemania game. Students match antonyms, synonyms, typical references, and definitions to all of the vocabulary words they have been studying. Directions to Puzzlemania can be found in chapter 2.

The first team to complete the Amazing Race wins ten house points; second place wins eight; third place, five; and fourth place, three.

TIPS for an Amazing Amazing Race:

- Inform students that the key ingredient in winning the Amazing Race is communication.
- Set up the game so teams will each run a different race (to avoid teams from just following one another).
- Ask permission before hanging a clue envelope outside a classroom or room. I often try to use spaces like the main office, library, art room, nurse's office, and cafeteria. The envelope is always placed outside the location so teams are not going into a space and disturbing a class in session.
- Send out a school-wide email, letting everyone know what your class will be doing, and check with the office to make sure there aren't any drills or other special activities taking place during the time of your Amazing Race.
- To prevent students from wreaking havoc in school halls, have them wear bracelets (made from pipe cleaners) and tell them that if any adult catches them running or behaving inappropriately, they must turn over their bracelet to the adult. For each person who returns without a bracelet, a one-minute penalty is subtracted from their time.
- Make fake envelopes to use as decoys and place cards inside with letters on them. This will deter students from just looking for envelopes rather than trying to solve the riddles.
- To get students excited, watch an episode of *The Amazing Race* with your students before they participate in your Amazing Race.

Building relationships with your students not only changes your how you relate to them; it changes your teaching. It gives a depth and meaning to your life that you with carry with you throughout your entire career.

Educator Spotlight: Connection Creates Change

A few years ago, I had a student named Britney. She was not a difficult student, but she did keep a wall up early on in the school year. I knew she was battling other issues, so I checked in on her often. I also noticed she would be writing, and not just about our lesson or what we were doing in class that day. One day, I kept her after class to talk to her about how she was doing and, more importantly, what she is always writing about. Britney told me she was writing raps and that she wanted to be a rapper. I said, "Great!" and told her that I wanted her to write raps about what we were learning in class. She excitedly agreed.

I gave Britney the class notes and told her to work on only this and nothing else. The very next day, she came in with a cassette tape (this was a while back) and handed it to me. I played the tape for our class, and it was incredible. She wrote an entire song about everything we were discussing in class, with a beat and backing vocals, and I was blown away. Needless to say, Britney got an A. I asked her to do it again for the next chapter, and she did. Britney went from failing my class to getting As on every test; she was memorizing the content, but in her own way.

Ten years later, Britney messaged me on social media and sent me a link to a recent interview she did on the radio after her first song aired. Britney went from writing raps to writing historical raps and is now a successful rapper and entertainer who works with Spotify. I am so proud of this amazing young lady,

but Britney just reinforced that so many of our students may be gifted in a way that may not be conventional, but that we can apply to our lessons to set them up for success.

**Nicholas Ferroni,
high school teacher**
@nicholasferroni

ACTION!

1. What are three things you can do to build lasting relationships with your students?

2. How can you show students they are the heart of your classroom environment?

3. Think of one lesson you teach that you could turn into a story.

4. How might teams or the house system help improve the culture of your class? What would be the first steps you'd take to create a system like that?

5. What academic content can you use to create an Amazing Race for your students?

CHAPTER FIVE

Mary Poppins

Beyond the Classroom Walls

Mary Poppins: the magical nanny who takes the Banks children on a series of unforgettable adventures to show them the magic in the world all around them. While most of us didn't have a nanny, we probably all remember our favorite babysitters. When I was about eight years old, my parents had the teenage boy across the street look after me when they had to work but school was closed. He was cool because he always took me out of the house: we went bike riding, bowling, and to the movies. It was great having experiences out in the world instead of just sitting at home. As teachers, it can be fun to take our students on adventures outside the walls of our classrooms, too.

"What's your favorite restaurant?" I asked my students that question over a decade ago. We went back and forth, debating which restaurants had better food, if McDonald's was better than Burger King, if the service at restaurant A was better than at restaurant B. Then a light-bulb went off in my head. It was a perfect opportunity to combine my favorite pastime of dining out with teaching math. Our next math unit would be on finding percentages—what could be a better experience then taking the kids out to dinner and having them put those new math skills to the test?

I contacted a local restaurant and explained what I wanted to do. I wanted to bring my entire class out to dinner and have them practice calculating the tax and tip. The parents would also be there (I didn't want to be solely responsible for twenty-five fifth graders), which would be a great opportunity to build relationships with them a week before our parent-teacher conferences. The owner graciously offered us the back room of the restaurant and created a special menu just for us.

The day of the dinner, students practiced how to use percentages to calculate both tax and tip. I then gave them an entire rundown of how the evening would work. First, I asked students to dress to impress. We talked about what appropriate attire would look like, and I asked that they try their hardest to look sharp. Next, we discussed what behaviors we should demonstrate, including how to order from a menu, saying "please" and "thank you," speaking at an appropriate volume, and so on. Students learned that when they entered the restaurant, they were to first introduce me to their parents (even if I already knew them) and then find a table. I explained that they would not be playing musical chairs, so they should choose their seats carefully. This was such a successful event that it became a tradition for years.

It's not always possible to bring a class out to dinner, and sometimes students may be unable to get to a dinner, but we can still create special memories for our students. In lieu of going to a restaurant, bring the restaurant to them. With a few tablecloths purchased from the dollar store, a handful of battery-operated candles, and dimmed lights, it's easy to transform your classroom into a restaurant. Students can choose their own seats, bring their own food, and pretend to be at their favorite restaurant. Another idea is to bring your students outside for a picnic. Ask them to bring in beach towels or old blankets and find a place on your school campus to dine al fresco. Students can also bring in game boards, and you can make an afternoon of it. This is a great alternative when parents may be unable to take students places after school.

Student Voice:
Expectations and Connection

When asked about my time in Mr. Butler's class, the first thing that came to mind was the way he made his students feel. His ability to cultivate and maintain genuine connections with every student who walked into his classroom was, and still is, inspiring to watch.

Connection is, in my experience, critical to being a great teacher. Mr. Butler does not care where you come from; what matters to him is that he helps you get where you're meant to go. His knack for making students feel comfortable and safe provides the framework for a positive environment for students to learn and grow. Mr. Butler makes learning—dare I say it—fun. I remember when he planned movie nights after school for our class and our families!

The movies were always adaptations of books we had read in class, which allowed us to learn something, as well. While he loves to form relationships and have fun, there is always a method to Mr. Butler's madness. Spending time and building connections with his students allows him to understand their likes, dislikes, and their styles of learning. And, while he makes learning fun, he also lays out a clear expectation of success. Mr. Butler's expectations are high because he knows his students are capable. When someone believes in you, it makes you want to be better, too.

James, class of 2009

Another favorite activity outside of the classroom is a movie night. I try to get a heads-up on a novel that will be coming out as a movie. We read the novel in class and then, as a celebration for finishing the book, we meet at the movie theater and watch the movie together. Ninety percent of the time, the kids realize the book is better than the movie (no offense, Hollywood), and the next day we do a little comparison of the movie and the book. The first time I did this was with *Bridge to Terabithia* by Katherine Patterson. It's my all-time favorite book, and seeing the movie with my students was magical. Other books we've seen as movies are *Mr. Popper's Penguins, Narnia, Hoot,* and *Wonder.*

Again, we don't need to physically take our students out into the world to create magical learning experiences for them. When going to an actual movie theater isn't an option, bring the movie to the students! School multipurpose rooms, libraries, or cafeterias are perfect places to use as theaters. I have also used my own classroom by moving student desks to the side, arranging the seats into rows, and setting up a movie-style screen using a queen-sized sheet and hooking my laptop up to an LCD projector.

In 2006, one of my favorite Disney movies, *Mary Poppins,* opened as a musical on Broadway. I went to see it for my twenty-fifth birthday and ever since have wanted to take my class to experience the magic, too. For the first few years, tickets were super expensive and hard to get, but finally in 2010, the production offered discounted group rates. I quickly polled the students parents' to see if they would be interested in venturing into Manhattan on a Sunday afternoon to see a performance. With more than half the class saying yes, I picked a date and ordered fifty tickets.

Clearly, it was a huge perk living less than an hour away from New York City. Not only was theater available, but we could get into Manhattan by either public transit or car. But you don't need to take your kids to Broadway to see live theater. Most cities and towns have local theater, and if that isn't an option, try meeting your kids at a college or high school performance. Not only is local theater entertaining; it's often affordable. Reaching out to a local theater, place of worship, or school, you may even be able to get your students complimentary tickets to shows at off times or during a preview/dress rehearsal. One of the many cool things about live theater (whether Broadway or a local downtown theater), there are almost always discount tickets for students and/or school groups—just ask.

Now living in Los Angeles, there are tons of beautiful hikes within a ten-mile radius of where I live. I'm always hiking, and it's something students know I do. Not everything I do beyond the classroom doors has to specifically tie into academics; learning to appreciate nature is a pleasure in itself, and many of us use nature as part of self-care. So, a few years ago, I planned a class hike. We met at the hike's trailhead on a Saturday morning. Like our other outings, a parent or guardian had to accompany each child. This is such an easy (and free) way to build those relationships. I think the parents appreciate these outings as much as the kids do, and as the teacher, I get insight to my students that I would never garner inside the walls of our classroom.

I'm a huge Barry's Bootcamp fan. I work out at Barry's four times a week, and my students know how much I enjoy it. In case you haven't heard of Barry's, it's a group exercise gym. A one-hour fitness class led by a Barry's instructor is billed as the best workout in the world, and I am a believer. My students know how much I like Barry's—but that workout is for adults only. However, during Covid, I had an idea. Everyone was stressed and underexercised, so I asked one of my favorite Barry's instructors if he would do a Zoom class with my kids. He said yes, and even spent his out time designing a class just for them. For thirty minutes, we logged onto Zoom, and my whole class got to experience a Barry's Bootcamp workout. This was free, and we didn't even need to leave the comfort of our living rooms! This is now my newest tradition. I now do it in class and my fitness instructor is kind enough to continue donating his time to stream fitness into our classroom via Zoom. But of course, you don't need a Barry's instructor to do a fitness class. Instead, ask your school's PE teacher or a parent to run a class. The excitement of someone different in the room makes it a special experience.

I'm constantly looking for ways to connect what students are learning in class to the real world. (Yes, I was the student who constantly asked the teacher, "Why are we learning this?" and "When would we ever actually use this?") As teachers, we are exposing kids to so much content that won't be useful in their real lives. I think that's why the television show *Are You Smarter than a Fifth Grader?* was such a success. As adults, we forget a lot of what we were taught in school. Not because we weren't taught it in the first place or it wasn't taught to us well, it's because we never needed to use that knowledge outside of the classroom.

Figuring out averages is a math skill that students will actually have to use in the "real world," but students hate doing it because it requires so much calculation. Adding up all the numbers, then using long division . . . how dull! The problems in math textbooks are too similar and usually involve the amount of precipitation in cites around the US. Unless you find that rare student who has a *real* passion for rain, no one is going to care about the average amount of rainfall in Albuquerque in June 2009. I've tried to connect averages to baseball, but mathematically that's tricky and goes far beyond the fifth grade learning standards. After I thought and thought about it, it finally clicked: Bowling! Calculating a bowling average was easy. We could do that in one outing. So, there I was, back at it, planning another classroom trip, this time to the bowling alley.

The first time I did this lesson, I planned it with my partner fifth grade teacher. The two of us visited the closest bowling alley and spoke to the manager. We explained we were teachers and wanted to bring students to the bowling alley for a math lesson. (If you haven't played the teacher card, please do. It works, and people feel good when they help kids out.) The manager said as long as we came in during an off time, he would give us a great deal—ten dollars for three rounds—then he threw in free shoe rentals.

We collected ten dollars from each student, and after school we met at the bowling alley for our "math lesson." After playing all three games, students had to calculate their own average, as well as their team's and the class's average. In addition to "doing math," we had a great time and also supported a local business. A win for everyone.

You do not need to take your class to the bowling alley. A lunchtime kickball game can serve the exact same purpose, namely, to create a time to build memories outside the regular classroom routine. Or if you really want to go bowling, try working with your school's PE teacher to set up your own bowling alley in the gymnasium or cafeteria. Students can take turns keeping score, setting up pins, and returning bowling balls.

Student Voice: Building Memories

One of my favorite memories from elementary school is when the class went to a family fun center to play laser tag, compete in mini-golf, and ride go-karts. It was a lot of fun to be with our class outside of school, because that was something not a lot of teachers would do with their students. Our parents and siblings were invited. My mom couldn't go, but Mr. Butler let my friend's mom take me. It was also fun because I hung out with people I normally would not have played with after school. I remember it was dark when we left, and the next day was our big house feast to celebrate the winning house. Even though my house of Coragem didn't win, it was still a lot of fun rooting on my friends.

Bryanna, class of 2013

A favorite end-of-the-year activity is taking my students go-karting at a local family fun center. When I taught in New York, we would do this the evening before our house banquet. Families were invited, and, again for a special price, we had two hours to roam the park with access to mini-golf, go-karts, and laser tag. If you want to build relationships with students, challenge them to a go-kart race. There's no mercy, just lots of laughs and fond memories. Since this was a family event, siblings of my students were often present. It was an easy way to spend time with former students, plus meet possible future students.

When it wasn't possible to go go-karting, I would invite students to meet me at the local frozen yogurt shop in our town. Not everyone would be able to go, but usually about half the class would show up, and we would enjoy frozen yogurt and talking together. In addition to spending time with my students, I also got to talk to parents in an informal setting, making connections with them, too. These outings are so important to teachers, because it's in the real world that we can form real relationships with our students and their families.

However, I'll admit that taking twenty-five fifth graders out into the real world isn't easy sometimes. And there are other ways to build those relationships outside the classroom walls. How about taking these ideas and tweaking them? Are you able to have students come in fifteen minutes early and, instead of going on a hike, walk around the perimeter of your school? Or bring the yogurt shop to them by setting up an ice-cream bar after lunch.

Other Ideas

Coffee Cafe. Dim the lights, turn on some jazz music, and let students drink hot cider, iced tea, or hot cocoa while they present a project, a poem, or do a book talk.

Beach Day. Invite students to bring their beach towels and sunglasses to school and have a day at the beach! Put some ocean sounds on, project a beach scene up on the wall, spray some suntan lotion around for the scent. Students can bring a bagged lunch or snack and eat a picnic lunch together.

Camp Out. See if any of your students, friends, or neighbors have tents you can borrow. Move the desks to the side of your classroom and set up some tents for students to work in. Lower the lights, play some cricket sound effects on your classroom speaker, and project a campfire up on the board. Feeling extra adventurous? Serve some s'mores and tell a ghost story.

Educator Spotlight:
Classroom Culture at First Glance

When you walk into our classroom, you'll notice three things: (1) the word "FAMILY" on our main wall (2) books upon books and (3) framed pictures of every student's family in our classroom.

One thing that often goes unnoticed is our class mailbox. It's arguably the most important tool we have. In order to continue to make our classrooms student-centered, I believe it's important to get feedback from the people who spend the most time with us: our students. But when is there time? In an era where teachers are given yet another task or another workbook to use, adding feedback seems insurmountable—but it's possible. In my classroom, we have our mailbox to help with that. Its purposes are many: notes from home, celebrations or concerns, and idea-sharing. Oftentimes, I'll receive uplifting sticky notes about how happy students are. Other times, students will share their worries. It's thanks to this mailbox that I've slowed down my teaching, moved one student away from another, received positive comments, and much more. This year is the first year I've used my mailbox, but I wish I would've thought of it sooner!

When I said you'll see books upon books when walking into our classroom, that's an understatement. You'll see wall-to-wall, head-to-toe, everything covered in books. I use books for everything: read-alouds, monthly classroom themes, science, and even math! (When you teach measurement and calculating perimeter and area, use books!)

My first classroom had only three rows of books, mostly from my childhood. Now you'll see more than seven full bookshelves covered in chapter and picture books, and my collection continues to grow. But it didn't happen overnight. Teacher book grants, gifts from friends, discount stores like Goodwill, and websites like DonorsChoose (my personal favorite) have truly helped to give my students access to relevant, new, and award-winning books. I read to my students daily, and I show them what book I'm currently reading. Most importantly, I give my students time to read every day.

If you show your students that books are important to you, you'll be amazed at the effects. Books have changed my life, and I hope they'll change my students lives, too—this year and beyond.

Jordan Potrzeba,
fourth grade teacher
@jordanpotrzeba

ACTION!

1. Brainstorm three ideas to strengthen bonds through making memories outside of your classroom walls.

2. Make a list of at least three local businesses that may support you in hosting your class in a special after-school activity. Commit to calling at least one of these businesses today.

3. What after-school activities might you be able to attend? These include any student sporting games, dance recitals, musical performances, or art exhibits your students have mentioned.

CHAPTER SIX

Coach Carter

Routines, Procedures, and Expectations

C oach Ken Carter returns to his California high school to coach the school's basketball team. His tough rules and academic discipline help his students and players succeed on the court, but when he notices their grades beginning to suffer, he shuts them out of the gym—and out of their chance of winning the championship. Despite being heavily criticized by his players and their parents, Coach Carter doesn't give up on making sure his players can do just as well in the classroom as on the basketball court.

I'm often asked how I am able to do all of these out-of-the-box lessons and activities with my class and still be able to get through all of the curriculum. Well, it's all about the subtitle of this chapter: routines, procedures, and expectations. From the first day of school, we define and practice the classroom's routines, procedures, and expectations. It's not something we go over once, but something we practice over and over again until we master it. It usually takes the entire first month of school before I can begin to let go of the reins and let the class run itself.

While this isn't a book on classroom management, I want to share why I believe classroom management is such a vital ingredient in a successful school year. As I've mentioned before, students, parents, and colleagues often describe me as the teacher who "runs a tight ship," yet in the same sentence also describe me as "fun" and "creative." I guess I do run a strict classroom, if that means that students understand and follow the expectations I have for them. Kids want rules; kids respond to having boundaries. There's no way I can turn the classroom into a candy factory without students understanding there are routines, procedures, and expectations to follow.

All of this means that in October, I stop being in charge and the kids run the classroom on their own. I love October. For example, I do not keep track of students going to the bathroom. Who has time to track bathroom use? During the first month of school, I teach students when the appropriate and inappropriate times to use the bathroom are. Students understand that at the beginning of a lesson, during direct instruction, or when independent reading, they may not leave the classroom. At the same time, students also are taught they do not need to ask permission or raise their hand to excuse themselves. When in the real world do you need to raise your hand or sign out to use the restroom? Other schools have their own policies for bathroom use, and I am not encouraging anyone to disregard those procedures, but what I am saying is that giving students the respect of knowing when and when not to use the bathroom will save you countless interruptions.

Recently, my principal's son was in my class. My principal and his wife (who is also a teacher) shared that he tells them every detail of what we do during the day. My first thought was that I'd better be *extra* careful what I do this year, and second, I wondered if this classroom mole meant I would be excused from observation that year. In all seriousness, the one thing my principal said was that the kids in my class this year still can't believe they are able to go to the bathroom without asking permission. That at first the kids thought I was tricking them. At the time I wrote this chapter, we had been in school for three months, and I had not had a single issue with students using the bathroom. I also hadn't been interrupted during teaching by a student asking to use the bathroom or had to speak to a student for using the bathroom at an inappropriate time. When students understand the reasoning behind your routines, procedures, and expectations, management problems are generally lessened.

Much as I love October, I am not a fan of September. If truth be told, I don't even like the first day of school. No one knows what is going on yet! I make it fun: students are magically placed into one of four houses, we play lively getting-to-know-you challenges, and all students start with a clean slate for what (I tell them) will be their best school year yet. But it's tough at first when kids don't know where things are, where to put things, where to go, how to do this or that, and don't yet know classroom expectations or my own pet peeves. How wonderful would it be for the students to come to school on the first day, already knowing all the routines, procedures, and expectations.

Anyone who says these can be taught on the first day—or even in the first week—has never been a classroom teacher. It takes time, and it's worth it.

It takes a solid month of school to get my students to the place where they are independent with our classroom routines. Every teacher

knows what their ideal expectations, routines, and procedures would be—that's up to you to determine. But no matter what you decide, implementing the accompanying behaviors is all about practice, practice, practice. And as tedious as it is for that first month . . . it makes the next nine months blissful.

TIPS for Back to School:

- Visually display your classroom expectations in your classroom.
- Model the behavior you expect.
- Practice procedures over and over again until students become independent.
- Share your expectations with the other teachers your students spend time with.
- Share your expectations with your students' families.

When teaching students your procedures and expectations, it's important to begin by building trust with them. You can't say something and then not follow through. If you are going to hold students accountable for something, now is the time to be very clear about expectations. Work ethic and neatness are both very important to me, and students should know that from the jump. We spend weeks talking about how I expect work to look and that their previous teacher's expectations are not mine. We go over examples of what class notes should look like, how to write on loose-leaf paper, how to set up a heading. We also talk about email etiquette and how to properly format and send emails to teachers and classmates. They also know that when work does not meet the expectations, they will do it over.

Please do not think the first month of school in my classroom is like boot camp! It's actually the opposite. We are consistently practicing things and have lots of discussions on how to react or what to do if you are asked to recomplete an assignment. Students understand that someone in the room will be the first person to have to recomplete work, and we discuss what that is going to feel like before it happens.

Once, I was in a meeting where one of the sixth grade teachers mentioned that one of my students said that if work wasn't done neatly in Mr. Butler's class, he would throw it out and make you do it again. The principal, who was in the meeting, said, "You don't really do that, right?" I said, "Absolutely, I do." Why would I threaten to throw out someone's messy work and then not follow through? Students would only learn that Mr. Butler isn't telling the truth and actually *will* accept messy work. It's not a big ordeal; no one yells or cries. I simply go over, take the work from the student, and politely ask them to do it again. Quite simple, no drama at all. And usually after someone is asked to redo an assignment once, it doesn't happen again. It's part of managing a classroom with high expectations.

Teachers know kids are smart. Kids know when they have earned an A and when they have been given an A. Deep down, we all want to earn As, not be handed them. Think back to some of your favorite teachers, the ones who really made you work for things. My junior year math teacher was one of these. I hated math in high school. Saw no purpose for algebra or calculus. I knew I wanted to be an elementary teacher, and nothing I was being taught in my final year of math class was ever going transfer over to what I would be doing in the real world. I let my teacher know that, too, informing him that I was fine with earning Bs in his class.

Luckily for me, he wasn't fine with that. He pushed me and helped me earn As, whether I wanted them or not. He spent countless hours before class and after class helping me. I now realize that it would have been much easier for him to have just given me an A, but he didn't, and that's why I remember him. Not every teacher is willing to go the extra mile like that. For example, my physics teacher back then was the opposite. Maybe he was close to retirement, maybe he had other things going on that we didn't know about, but at the end of the day, we knew he just didn't care and none of us respected him. Yeah, we loved being able to do the minimal amount of work, but he taught the class for one reason: to pass the New York State Regents. That's all that mattered, and we knew it. It was "kill and drill" until the day of the test. I barely passed that exam.

Walking the Line

Kids want boundaries. People (for the most part) respect boundaries. In my class, I give an entire lesson to my students about what I call "the line." I tell students that we will frequently be having a good time in class, but we must respect "the line." We talk about what "the line" is and how we can get close to it, but that there will be consequences for crossing it. We discuss what crossing "the line" looks like and what the consequences will be. Every teacher will have their boundaries, but kids should know what those are and what will happen if they cross them.

Student Voice:
Expectations Add Support

In fifth grade, I really remember that we always knew what to do because everything was always explained clearly. Mr. Butler never had to yell at the class, and no one ever got in trouble. I also liked that we had time in our day to catch up on work or get extra help with anything we didn't understand. Mr. Butler would help people at the back table so they wouldn't have to take things home for extra homework. Something else we did a lot of was work in groups or with partners. When we worked in groups, Mr. Butler gave each person a specific job so that everyone was responsible for getting the project finished.

Karlee, class of 2015

We also practice such things as how to participate, turn in work, walk from class to class, and ask for help. I teach students that they are responsible for a few things when participating in class. The first being they need to stand or position their body to face the majority of the class. The art of standing, eye contact, and commanding an audience is a life skill that goes way beyond just classroom participation. By standing or positioning their body toward the audience, students' voices can be better heard, it's easier for other students to make eye contact with the speaker, and students gradually become more comfortable speaking to an "audience." Students also are taught that while standing, they should maintain eye contact with their peers and position their body so they are facing as many people as possible. This is a practice my entire fifth grade team does, and over the school year, they become confident public speakers.

After the first few weeks of school, I also do not walk my students to and from class. Of course, it wouldn't be appropriate for kindergartners to be walking around the school by themselves—and every school is set up differently, with different rules and teacher expectations. If you as a teacher are expected to walk your students to class, then please continue to do so. I do, however, encourage you to open up a conversation about the why behind walking older students around. Is it possible for them to be taught to move from class to class on their own? If so, then try it. But before doing so, set students up for success. This is also a skill that needs to be practiced. Seventy-five percent of the time, I do not walk my students from class to class. They are expected to be able to gather their materials and get to their next class on time. Twenty-five percent of the time, I might join them (usually if I need to go somewhere as well) and observe how they are transitioning around campus.

Another two things I've incorporated in my classroom come from my friend Adam Dovico and his books *The Limitless School* and *When Kids Lead* (coauthored by Todd Nesloney). The first is Adam's acronym SPECIAL:

- S–Shake hands (or some other kind of greeting)
- P–Posture/body language
- E–Eye contact
- C–Charm
- I–Introductions
- A–Ask questions
- L–Listen

SPECIAL helps students with their personal presentation skills. Teachers are often told that we are preparing our students for jobs that do not yet exist, but being able to communicate is a skill everyone benefits from learning.

Our fifth graders go through SPECIAL training and are expected to use these skills when interacting with others or giving presentations. It's something many of the teachers in my school have adopted and has even sparked a leadership elective. I recommended reading Adam and Todd's book to get specific ideas on how to teach these skills, especially the art of charm.

The second of Adam's ideas my team and I have incorporated is that of classroom ambassadors. Our student ambassadors were inspired by the ambassador program Adam created at his own school and wrote about in *When Kids Lead*. When creating our new leadership electives, we felt our student leaders should have specific responsibilities around our school's campus. Our student ambassadors are responsible for greeting visitors throughout our classrooms, school, and during large campus-wide events. They use their SPECIAL skills to help people feel welcome at our school. For larger events, like our school-wide assemblies, our ambassadors wear shirts to identify themselves, so anyone with a question or issue can find them easily. And during weekly meetings, ambassadors practice the art of communication, learning how to greet people and ask questions and follow-up questions. We discuss the importance of body language and first impressions.

In March 2020, when the world halted and we moved from teaching in person to distance learning, one of the reasons why I think my students were able to adapt so well is because of the expectations that had been set for them. I was in some ways fortunate to have one of the best classes of students I ever taught (though it was disappointing that I couldn't finish the year out with them in person, as some of my favorite lessons come during the latter part of the year). In the two and a half months we were on Zoom together, I never once had a problem with student engagement, attendance, or incomplete work. I was fortunate in that I didn't have any students that year with extreme or challenging home situations, but I also think that holding my students accountable from day one made a difference in the behavior they displayed on Zoom.

Every school has its own unique challenges, and giving students full rein to run the classroom may not be part of your school's culture. That's okay. When I taught at the start-up school, we shared a campus with three other schools. Allowing kids to walk around that campus on their own was not a possibility by any means. For those two years, I did walk students from class to class, and that worked well, but I gave them other privileges within our own classroom. And when I taught in New York, the school required teachers to keep track of when students left the classroom. For those years, I had a little sign-out sheet at the classroom door where students signed out and jotted down where they were going. But, while the rules in my classrooms might have varied, setting boundaries and expectations kept things running smoothly for the entire year.

Educator Spotlight:
School Is for the Students

I spent my entire life at summer camp. From junior counselor to program director, I held practically every role at camp. Something our senior leadership team constantly shared with our staff is: "Camp is for the campers." A staff member would be upset that they were not chosen to lead the activity. Camp is for the campers. A staff member was hurt because their crush broke their heart. Camp is for the campers. This little saying would change an entire situation in seconds. When I made the decision to embark on a career in education, the leadership skills I developed at summer camp formed the foundation of what it means for me to lead in school. "Camp is for the campers" quickly became "School is for the students."

Our public education system is facing more challenges now than ever before. From a national labor shortage that is creating insurmountable staffing challenges to closing the gaps from a never-ending pandemic, it has been tough to say the least. However, in my most challenging moments, I say to myself, "School is for the students." Challenging conversation with a coworker? School is for the students. Difficult email from a student's family? School is for the students. Want to hit that snooze button in the morning? School is for the students. Our kids are urgently in need of strong leadership. It is so easy to lose track of our why, especially given all we are currently experiencing as educators. But

remembering that "School is for the students" helps me stay grounded in my ultimate mission, which is ensuring every student has the equitable, high-quality education they deserve.

Kyle Cohen, fourth grade teacher
@mr.kylecohen

ACTION!

1. Quickly write down your classroom rules and expectations. Think of ways to set up students for success when teaching these procedures and routines.

2. In what ways can you give your students a sense of ownership in setting your classroom expectations for the year?

3. How do you follow through when students do not adhere to classroom expectations?

4. Is there a clearly defined "line" in your classroom? Do students know how to keep from crossing it?

5. In what ways are you able to incorporate teaching communication skills, such as personal presentation and speaking skills, into your curriculum? If the "SPECIAL" acronym doesn't work for your classroom, what word could you use? What would each letter stand for?

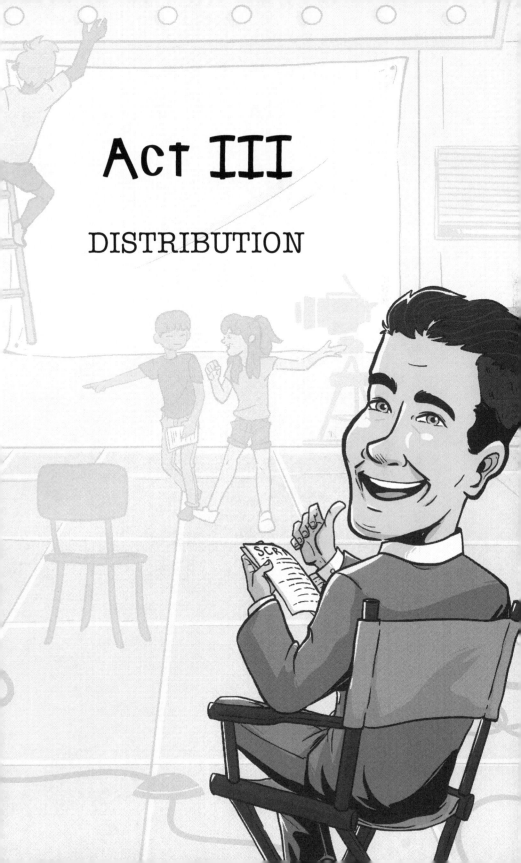

Act III

DISTRIBUTION

CHAPTER SEVEN

Willy Wonka and the Chocolate Factory

Classroom Design

Who can forget the first time they saw *Willy Wonka and the Chocolate Factory* (the original 1971 version with Gene Wilder) and the moment when the children first enter Willy Wonka's factory? For a child, it was mind-blowing to see the edible world Willy Wonka created. That's how I want my students to feel every day when they walk into our classroom. (Willy Wonka was not only a candy genius; his candy factory was proof that he was also an art director!)

My very first classroom was in a portable trailer. There was absolutely nothing fancy about it, but it was mine. At twenty-two years old, I didn't have a lot of money, so I made do with what I had. Most of my money was spent on books for my classroom library. And while it certainly didn't look like my castle-themed classroom of today, I absolutely loved it and so did the kids.

There are two strong opinions about classroom decor. There are people who are against it, and people who are all out for it. Within the latter group, there are opinions on the amount of student work that should be hung up, with some claiming that too many decorations are distracting for students. But as I mentioned before, every school has their own rules and limitations on what teachers can and cannot create in their space. In New York, we were not allowed to have anything hanging from ceilings. I tried repeatedly, but it never lasted for more than a few days. Finally, I got creative and asked if the school could install art wires that would be anchored one foot *below* the ceiling (we had really high ceilings) so that the wire would stretch across the classroom in a zig-zag design. After that, I was able to hang things and not break the rules; all it took was getting a little creative in my thinking. So remember: you are the art director of your classroom.

Student Voice:
Classroom Transformation

Fifth grade was one of those school years I will never forget. Mr. Butler would transform the entire classroom to reflect the lesson of the day. With all the colors, music, and costumes, it seemed more like a movie set than a classroom most of the time. Another memory I have is all the fun games we played to help us learn better. This made Mr. Butler's class so unique. He always went the extra mile to make things as interactive and fun as possible. And it worked: each day we would go home and think about what the next day of class would bring. This anticipation only immersed us more into the learning experience and showed us that school could be a place where you could have fun but also be productive at the same time.

Nick, class of 2012

TIPS on Buying Classroom Decor:

1. Set and stick to a budget. Each year I add one "extra special" item to my classroom.

2. Shop at secondhand stores, yard sales, and on Craigslist. Before paying, tell them you're a teacher and the items are for your classroom.

3. Set up an Amazon Wish List and upload a proposal on DonorsChoose.

4. If you have a classroom budget, use that money on consumables; save your own money for items that you want to keep long-term. This is also useful in the event you leave the school; your decor items will be your personal property that you can take with you.

5. Ask parents to help. For example, my house wheel was built and donated by a student's parent. Students spin this wheel each Friday for a chance to win bonus house points.

As teachers, we want our students to enter our classrooms and be comfortable. This also means that we ourselves need to be comfortable in our own spaces. My classroom at the moment is designed to look like what I call a "modern-day castle." There are faux-stone wall coverings on the walls, flame-style lamps, a fireplace (that I built from scratch), a small stage (that a very generous carpenter built for me), a classroom library, and tons of photos of my current and former students.

What I will tell you is that my students instantly know how much I care about the space we learn in. While I have been very fortunate to have A LOT of my classroom decor and furniture donated to me by parents, local businesses, or websites like DonorsChoose, I have also spent a lot of my own money. But honestly, you do not need to spend your own money to be a successful teacher or have a great classroom. And of course I wish schools would give teachers bigger classroom budgets to create warmer and friendlier spaces, but I have never worked in a school that offered more than $250 a year to set up my classroom. Not nineteen years ago, not today. $250 divided by 24 kids gives me about $10.40 a student. What does that fund? Pretty much

nothing. In New York, however, our parent-teacher organization gave each classroom teacher a very generous gift card to the local school supply store. That was extremely helpful, as you might imagine!

As teachers, many of us have become accustomed to begging and bartering for resources and classroom materials. I pull out my teacher card everywhere I go. Okay, it's not a literal card—but I always ask for teacher discounts anytime I buy something for my classroom, and usually I am able to get one. Whether it be 10 percent or 50 percent, people generally feel for teachers. I recently wanted to surprise my class with donuts, because they'd all reached a recent goal we set. In Los

Angeles, we have this cool donut shop called Randy's Donuts. They've been in business since the 1950s and are a staple here. But their donuts are expensive! I could have just gone to the grocery store and bought donuts (which I sometimes do), but I wanted these to be extra special.

So, when I went in, I pulled out the teacher card. I asked the twentysomething behind the counter if they gave teacher discounts (knowing they didn't), and he said no. I explained my class recently met a goal we were working on and how I wanted to surprise them with these awesome donuts. The employee told me if I came back in a few hours, he could give me donuts at 50 percent off, but not to tell anyone. I eagerly smiled and told him I would be back. Pretty soon, I had two dozen really amazing donuts sitting in my car, and instead of spending thirty-three dollars on them (I told you they were expensive), I spent sixteen dollars.

Not every person or store will be willing or able to give you a 50 percent discount, but I welcome and appreciate even the smallest of discounts. It never hurts to ask local businesses for help. Like I mentioned before, I am not a fan of the first day of school—but that doesn't interfere with my making the day as special as possible. This year I wanted balloons, like BIG BALLOONS. I wanted the room to look extra special after eighteen months of distance learning. So, I contacted a local party business who creates truly awesome balloon displays. Well, this business really went out of their way to make the first day of school extra special for my students. I originally asked for one of their "famous" balloon bouquets mixed with the four colors of our houses, but instead they sent four GIGANTIC balloon bouquets, one for each house! Not only did they donate these incredible balloon bouquets, but they refused to let me pay for delivery! When they arrived, I didn't even know if I could fit them through my classroom door. I had to separate their masterpieces and ultimately shared the balloons with the other fifth grade teachers to get them to fit. Since the business didn't want any recognition for their act of kindness, I quietly forwarded their name to our school so if we were ordering balloons in the future, we could send school business their way. My class also sent the owner thank-you cards and told them how the balloons made their first day back to school extra special. Relationships matter.

A few years ago, classroom stages became the big social media trend. I wanted a stage so badly, but I didn't know how to build one. I searched online for local carpenters and once again pulled out my teacher card. I found someone who was willing to create the stage I wanted, and all I would have to fund was the lumber, not the labor. As a contractor, he already got a discount on the lumber, so for under a hundred dollars he built me a beautiful classroom stage. Not only does this make my classroom "cool," it's amazing for student presentations. But of course, it's not necessary (or sometimes possible) to have a stage built for you. My teacher partner removed the legs from a sturdy coffee table she purchased from a secondhand store; it works perfectly as her classroom stage.

There is a wall with pictures of my current students and their family photos. On the first day of school, I ask students to bring in a current photo of their family. I enlarge the photos on a color copier and frame them with frames I buy at the dollar store. At the back of the room, in the classroom library, there is a wall displaying the covers of every book we read. By the end of the year, that wall will be covered with about 180 book covers. What you won't find in my classroom are bulletin boards. I used to have them, I used to change them, but now I've set up my classroom so that there's no need to change the decor every month.

I do, however, move desks around a lot. My general configuration stays the same, but I move seats frequently. It keeps kids on their toes and allows them to collaborate with different people. It's an easy way to switch things up.

Clip Art Classroom

There are schools that want classrooms to showcase student work. In lieu of displaying work on bulletin boards, each student has a clipboard. The clipboards hang from the front of my cabinets, and students clip their work to their clipboard. The newest masterpiece is on top, but their remaining work is safe underneath. Classroom visitors are able to see recent work and work from throughout the year.

In my classroom, you will also find a few inspirational sayings, lots of little teacher gifts I have received over the years (I never throw a student gift away). Gifts from my very first class are placed on my desk. They have sat on my desk for nineteen years, and I know exactly who gave me each one. There's a flower pen, a Kermit the Frog, a small globe, and lots of notes and cards tucked away in my desk organizer. The other gifts are displayed proudly above my desk, including a Dunder-Mifflin plaque a student gifted me a few years ago.

Dunder-Mifflin? Yes, I am a huge fan of the television show *The Office* and have probably seen every single episode a minimum of twelve times. Living in Los Angeles and working at an independent school, we get a lot of parent tour groups, and every now and again there will be a celebrity mixed into the group. I've become accustomed to it, and honestly, 95 percent of the time I don't recognize the celebrities who walk through. Once a real A-lister walked through, and I thought the person looked familiar. I thought it was maybe a neighbor of mine? It wasn't until lunch that I learned it was Charlize Theron.

Anyway, back to *The Office*, about five years ago, I was teaching a math lesson, and one of these tour groups walks through my room, and right in from of me was Jenna Fischer, aka Pam Beasley from *The Office*. I was speechless. There she was, right in front of me, watching me teach a math lesson. For thirty seconds I wanted to call out "PAM!"

But I refrained, conducted myself like a professional, and continued teaching. As she was leaving, she turned to me and said this was the coolest classroom she'd ever seen.

Your classroom doesn't need to look like a castle, it doesn't need a stage, a fireplace, or a dragon; what it does need is YOU! What kind of room would you love to teach in?

Top 10 Ideas for Classroom Decor and Ambiance

1. Classic movie or musical posters and book covers make great wall art.
2. An oversized rug or carpet (visit carpet stores and shop their clearance section).
3. A class pet. Try a betta fish, because all they need is a bowl and to be fed once every few days.
4. Houseplants (real or fake).
5. Take black-and-white photographs of places around your community. Enlarge them to poster size and hang them up around your room.
6. Comfy chairs or large pillows for students to sit on.
7. Floor or table lamps.
8. Holiday-style string lights (less expensive than LED strips).
9. An accent wall created with Fadeless paper rolls bought from craft or school supply stores.
10. A bulletin board covered with photos of your past and current students.

Educator Spotlight:
A Star Classroom Decorator's Tips

First-time guests open the door to our classroom, step inside, gasp as they look around, and say that it looks like a home or a trendy coffee shop, and it make me smile every time.

The words "We Are Family," with all the students' names intertwined, are proudly displayed as the focal point of our classroom. It's evident when you look around that this place is our "home away from home." We spend an average of seven hours a day here, so why not make it into a space that we are going to love, right?

My goal was to create a cozy, unique, aesthetically pleasing yet functional space that sparks creativity. In planning the space, I made sure to include the following essentials:

- Space to proudly display student work
- Easily accessible classroom library: all genres of books with a focus on diversity and inclusion
- Calm corner with access to comfortable seating, SEL resources, breathing cards, etc.
- Flexible seating: movable tables and a variety of seating options
- "Magic Carpet" area where I can gather my students for morning meetings and mini-lessons
- Elements of surprise, such as our prize wheel, candy machines, juke box, hidden green screen, tech station, comfy couch, small-group station, outdoor patio with convertible benches, and more
- Sufficient storage areas to hide all the cluttery "fun" stuff—classroom transformation bins and art supplies—to keep our space neat and organized

When asked to give advice to new teachers setting up their classrooms for the first time or to veteran teachers looking to refresh their space, I always share the following tips:

- Don't expect to do everything all at once. Just start with one bulletin board or wall at a time.
- Consider a color scheme or a theme that will not be too overstimulating or busy. You want to provide a calming space that will not become a distraction for your students.
- Sometimes less is more.
- Don't spend too much of your own money! Tap into all the resources such as your PTO/PTA, DonorsChoose projects, grants, donations, and items you find at garage sales that can be repurposed.
- Make it YOU! You don't have to imitate someone else's classroom you see on social media just because it's "pretty." Create a space that works for you and your learning community. You know your needs and preferences more than anybody else.
- Fill your space with LOVE! Please create a space where ALL of your students will feel welcomed, included, appreciated, and loved.

Nancy Chung, fifth grade teacher
@fancynancyin5th

ACTION!

1. What inspires you to make your classroom space welcoming to students?

2. How can you give students a say in the setup of your classroom?

3. Where do you get ideas for classroom decor and design from?

4. In what ways are you able to show-case photos of your former and cur-rent students?

5. List three local businesses, families, or friends you can get donations from to help with your classroom setup.

CHAPTER EIGHT

Meet the Parents

Parents

Just like Greg Focker was nervous to meet his girlfriend's family in *Meet the Parents*, we teachers often get nervous when meeting our students' parents. Fortunately, we can usually avoid the unfortunate series of events Greg faces when meeting his future in-laws.

The teacher-parent connection is a vital ingredient of what makes a strong school community. Some of the best advice I received as a teacher is that we must remember parents are trusting us with their most valuable asset: their child(ren).

As I mentioned earlier, every year at Back to School Night, I begin my presentation by thanking the parents for trusting me with their child(ren). I then go on to talk about how I truly believe it "takes a village." There is no way (at least I haven't found a way yet) to do what I do without the support of the parents of my students, and that relationship needs to be built beginning on the first day of school.

As I mentioned in the prologue, if I'd have stayed at my school in New York for one more year, there was a chance I could have been teaching an entire class of former students' siblings. That would have been pretty cool, because the relationships with those parents were already created and cultivated. Some of my closest friends are the parents of former students. I know that is looked down on at many schools (the school where I currently work frowns upon fraternizing with parents). However, when I first moved to Los Angeles, the first people to visit me were the parents of two former students who are brothers. That's meaningful community. I continue to receive holiday cards, birthday greetings, and dinner invitations from parents of former students. I've had parents of former students to my home, and I've had the privilege of being invited to some of my students' homes.

In *Go See the Principal*, author Gerry Brooks explains that communication between teachers and parents is not just important but is also a two-way street. Both parties must participate in communicating with each other.

My parent communication routine includes sending weekly updates about classroom happenings, updating Google Classroom, and publishing a monthly newsletter. But parents should also be active participants in the home-to-school communication. I encourage parents to respond to my emails, ask questions, and pass along information that may help me help their child. This includes when a family member is ill, if there are any changes in home situations, or anything else that may be different from the norm. I also encourage parents to reach out to me prior to going to the principal with a problem or issue. As difficult or awkward as it may be to call the teacher about an issue, it's so important to maintain the level of trust.

If possible, avoid communicating back and forth with parents over any student-related issue over email. I encourage parents to come in and meet in person, and if that's not possible, to schedule a phone call or Zoom meeting. And when meeting with a parent, the first thing I do is listen. As teachers, listening is so important. I give them all the time they need to voice their concerns and acknowledge their feelings. Before responding, I thank them for their time and tell them I appreciate that they reached out to me first. I respond to their concerns and then usually ask permission to speak to their child. I then invite them for a follow-up call (usually in about a week) to touch base again and discuss any changes, improvements, or ongoing issues. I would say 75 percent of the time, this works. Of course, there are times when the issue is larger and we may need to get a third party involved, which is fine, as long as it's communicated clearly, calmly, and with the best intentions. It's okay to require support in problem solving.

TIPS for Teacher-Parent Communication

- Weekly newsletters/email blasts. Keep parents in the know of what's been happening or what's planned for the upcoming week.
- Class website or Google site. These are relatively easy to build and can be updated as needed with classroom schedules, plans, parties, and performances.
- Seesaw. Similar to a website, but easier! Seesaw is a great way to show parents student work, as it can be used as a digital portfolio.
- Remind. A one- or two-way (up to you) communication app that allows you to send texts to your entire class, or just to individuals.
- Social media. Depending on your school rules, creating a social media page for your class can be a great way to keep your students' parents connected to what is happening in your classroom. It's important to keep the page private and only allow the parents of your current students access to the page.

When I take students on trips outside of the school day, the parents and/or other adult family members, such as aunts, uncles, and grandparents, are always invited (and often required) to attend. If a parent or family member is unable to attend, I try to match students up with a buddy so they can still participate in the activity. When planning trips, try to be sure your most challenging student or parent attends, because that can be a game changer in your relationship. The level of empathy and respect built during out-of-school experiences is big.

One of my favorite outings in New York was taking the kids to the Statue of Liberty. We tried doing this as a school field trip, but it required too tight of a schedule. My school was an hour outside of Manhattan, and on a bus, that was two hours or more in traffic. By the time we arrived at Battery Park, boarded the ferry, and got to the Statue of Liberty/Ellis Island, the day was too rushed. Cramming it all in was tough on kids and a burden for teachers who had families waiting for them at home.

But learning about twentieth-century immigration, the Statue of Liberty, and Ellis Island are meaningful parts of the social studies curriculum, and I *was* the social studies teacher. So, in lieu of squeezing this trip into a school day, I organized an optional weekend trip for my students and their families. We would meet at Battery Park on a Saturday morning. With no time constraints, we would then board the ferry and explore the Statue of Liberty and Ellis Island together like a big family, and then head to the South Street Seaport for dinner. Not everyone could come, but more than half did. I loved this trip not only because I appreciated the social studies aspect of it, but also because we were together, building bonds and creating memories that I knew these kids (and their parents) would remember for years to come.

The last time I did this trip was in June 2014, a week before I was to announce I was leaving New York and moving to California. After an incredible day, we (as always) walked down to the South Street Seaport to find a place to eat dinner. A few students and their families decided to head back home, but most of us walked our way to find dinner. When we arrived, two things happened.

The first, there was an art show. We weren't sure exactly what was being presented, but it vaguely looked like beautiful paintings created by local artists were on display. One of the parents wanted to take a class photo so we stood proudly and smiled—not realizing that we were standing in front of a dozen nude paintings of men and women. I wanted to die. There in the background of our beautiful photo were naked bodies! We laughed.

As if that weren't enough, across from the art show was a large candy store. To deflect attention from the nude paintings (and when I say nude, I mean *nude*, with detail), I invited everyone into the candy store. While browsing, a parent noticed a back room, and we meandered back there, finding a huge array of X-rated candy items. I was in shock. First nude paintings, now X-rated candy! A parent stood at the door of the back room, and I swiftly escorted any kids out. I was happy that I already had a new job lined up, three thousand miles to the west.

When I talk to those parents (which I still do, eight years later), we still laugh about that day. You couldn't have made it up. It was funny, memories were made, and bonds were created. Relationships matter.

We do not need to visit a national monument to create these special moments with families. One of my favorite ways to build community with parents is to invite them into the classroom for special activities and games. At the beginning of the year, try inviting parents to be guest readers and/or parent helpers. Kids love when their parents, grandparents, aunts, or uncles come to read a book to the class.

Later in the school year, I begin to host Scrabble tournaments. I ask for Scrabble board donations, and on Friday afternoons, parent volunteers come in to play Scrabble with the kids. This is so easy, and both the kids and parents love it. The parents help the kids play, keep score, and judge whether words are spelled correctly. I, as the teacher, don't have to do much, mainly walk from group to group, snapping photos and enjoying the engagement. If Scrabble isn't your thing, try other games, like Boggle or chess.

One year, we adopted a new math program to align to new math standards. At that time, I was receiving a lot of anxious parent emails, asking how they could help their children with this "new math." I understood; the struggle was real—I taught math for a living and sometimes had trouble figuring out this new way of thinking. So, we began having parent math days. Parents would join our math block and participate in a math lesson with their child.

I would choose days when the new concept was on the easier side, but I wanted parents to get a look at how the math was being explained. The real goal was for parents to feel empowered to help their children. This was not a "look at how hard this is" or a "gotcha" type of experience. A few days before parents would be coming in, I would send home the lesson with everything I would be teaching that day. This included every question, with an answer key and a sheet showing the work used to solve every single problem that would be presented that day. I wanted parents to be comfortable in my classroom and to feel that if their child needed their help, they would be able to offer it.

These parent math days were amazing to witness. I taught very little. I wanted to avoid putting myself in a position to be criticized. The point was to let parents get a glimpse of what their child's math class looked like, and then to actually do math with their child. It was a win-win for all. I did this this for years, even after parents (and I!) got used to the "new math."

Teachers and parents have to work together to create a successful school year. The more information we give them, the more likely they are to be willing to help us. Crucial point: The first time a parent hears from you, it should not be for something bad. When parents are used to hearing from you through previous emails, newsletters, phone calls, Zoom meetings, or text messages, they'll be much more likely to be on your side when you need to relay some challenging news.

Back to School Night

Back to School Night or Meet the Teacher Night can be a nerve-racking experience for teachers. While we are comfortable speaking in front a class of students, not all of us feel the same when speaking in front a group of adults. So, when meeting parents for the first time at Back to School Night, I try to keep it simple. I welcome them with a big smile and thank them for trusting me with their children. I show them a picture of myself as a fifth grader and tell them a little about my own childhood, as well as my educational and professional journey. I point out the things that make our classroom unique, go over major parts of our curriculum, and conclude with the expectations I have both for their children and for them as parents.

BTS Expectations Conversation: Hello, Parents!

1. My class is hard, but not impossible. I have high standards for your children, but with those high standards, I will do everything I can to help them not just meet expectations but surpass them.

2. I am human and make mistakes. I am not perfect. I have bad days, and if something ever seems off, please reach out right away. Please don't let things go—often an email or phone call can quickly clear up any miscommunications, misunderstandings, and my own mistakes.

3. Please bother me. That miscommunication could have been easily avoided by a quick conversation or email. However, I am working all day, so I do request the twenty-four-hour response rule. And emergencies, of course, should be reported to the school office.

4. We are a family. I truly believe that it takes a village. You will be asked to participate in some out-of-the box experiences, and I'm hoping you can lean in and embrace it.

5. (This one usually gets their attention.) Homework: there's not a lot of it. I don't like assigning homework. With the exception of math fluency and learning basic facts, e.g., multiplication and division, if a child can solve three multistep math problems correctly, there's no reason to do twenty of them. And if they can't do three, solving twenty isn't going to help. I will follow

---

the homework guidelines provided by my school, but homework assignments are meant to be brief and to review material taught in class.

6. However, I want students to READ. I encourage students to use their time after school to read for pleasure. I do not assign reading logs or give rewards for students who read at home. Reading for pleasure means reading whatever they like, including magazines, newspapers, graphic novels, and cookbooks or other how-to types of books.

7. Long-term projects. In lieu of worksheets, students will be assigned several long-term projects over the course of the year. Students will be able to complete most of the projects independently, but at-home support and help are always welcome. (I give a synopsis of the projects that students will be working on.)

And that's it! I end the evening by engaging parents in some type of game, such as the Classmate Search or Puzzlemania. I avoid taking questions, but instead ask parents to reach out to me personally with any questions or concerns they have (which helps me begin to create a relationship with my new students' families).

Long-Term/Home Projects

Long-term projects often include help from parents, but also, they are pivotal in teaching students how to manage their time. I believe this is an important skill for our students to learn. When I assign a long-term project, part of the directions is a suggested timeline, breaking down when certain parts of the project should be completed. I use the word "suggested" because we all tackle long-term projects differently. I also help students pinpoint what parts of the project they may need help with. While most students may be able to get help from their parents, it's important to understand that not all parents are available to help their children with school projects. As noted in the California State SEL Standards (as well as in many other states that have adopted SEL standards), students should feel supported in the classroom, community, and at home. I work with students to create a list of other people (generally adults) whom they can turn to for help. We also discuss that when asking people for help, we must do so in advance, and that it's important to plan ahead. In addition, I always include a scoring rubric so students (and parents) know exactly what is expected of them and how their project will be scored.

Fiction T-Shirt Project: Scoring Rubric			
Category	3–Extremely Well Done	2–Well Done	1–Additional Effort Needed
Presentation	Speaker spoke clearly, engaged the audience, maintained eye-contact and was well prepared.	Speaker spoke clearly and was able to be heard. Speaker read from their portfolio and had some eye-contact and engagement.	Some or all of he presentation was hard to understand. Speaker did not engage audience. Speaker depended on reading their portfolio.
Questions/ responses	Speaker was able to answer all questions with confidence.	Speaker was able to answer most questions with confidence.	Speaker was able to answer some of the questions and may have lacked confidence.
Completion	Al directions were followed and the project was submitted on time.	Most of the directions were followed and the project was submitted on time.	Some of the directions were not followed and/ or the project was submitted late.
T-shirt design	T-shirt looks professional. Contains words and unique design on the front and the back.	T-shirt looks neat. Contains words or designs on the front and the back.	Parts of the project lacks detail or neatness. Unique designs may be missing.
Persuasiveness	All of the l guidelines for persuasive writing were followed.	Most of guidelines for persuasive writing were followed.	Some of the guidelines for persuasive writing were followed.
Comments/Score:			

THE MILLION-DOLLAR MATH PROJECT

One of my favorite projects is called the Million Dollar Math Project. In the beginning of the year, after reviewing place value and number sense, students in my math class receive a mysterious envelope. Inside is a handwritten letter informing them that they have inherited a million dollars. BUT, in order to claim it, they must follow a strict set of criteria explaining how they must spend it:

1. Savings
2. College/Vocational school
3. Housing
4. Transportation (optional)
5. Family vacation
6. Charity donation
7. Other (big-ticket item of their choice)

Each topic has its own specific directions. For example, their home must cost less than $500,000 (no mega-mansions) and must currently be on the market. This is my favorite part to watch students research because they are in SHOCK how much homes cost, especially in their home city of Los Angeles. Almost all my students choose to relocate from Southern California to a more affordable area in order to buy a home that has everything they want and to stay within the project's budget. They must save for college or vocational school. If students decide not to go to college or vocational school, that money can be used to invest in a business or passion project. Students must also plan to take their family on a vacation, and therefore will have to research the price of travel expenses, food, hotels, and entertainment. After that, students find a charity to which they would like to donate money and must be prepared to explain the reasoning behind why they chose that particular charity. In addition, students must place money into a savings account and determinate how much interest (based on today's rates) they will have earned when they turn eighteen years old. Finally, students may spend any additional money on a "big-ticket" item. This could be installing a pool in the backyard of the home they bought, or anything else they have the funds for.

Students must then create a portfolio showing exactly how they have spent their million dollars, with the goal of getting to a balance of zero. They submit their portfolio, a recording sheet, and a reflection. Students present their project to the class, and if successful, I hand them a Hershey bar wrapped in a "million-dollar bill," a wrapper I created on the computer and print out on green paper.

Materials:

1. Directions
2. Sample portfolio
3. List of suggested resources, such as websites

Cost: $

Prep time: First time, several hours. After that, minimal.

Project duration: 2–3 weeks

Home support: Minimal. (I provide class time to work on this project, especially time to use the school computers and internet.)

ELL support: Offer your time to help students with portions of the project in school. If possible, provide directions for parents in the language that is spoken at home.

T-SHIRT ADVERTISEMENTS

Another fun project is the T-Shirt Book Project. Students choose a novel to read. My only two requests are that each child reads a different book and that the book they choose is not one they have read before. After students finish their book, in lieu of a boring book report, students must design, create, and then wear a T-shirt designed to persuade other students in the class (and school) to read the book. All shirts must be designed on a plain white T-shirt, and both sides of the shirt should be used for their walking advertisement. I encourage kids

to avoid using iron-ons and to draw as much as they can. Students know they will be wearing their T-shirts all day and should be proud of the attire they created. Similar to the Million Dollar Math Project, students present their T-shirts to the class by giving a short two-minute synopsis of their book (without giving away the ending) and tell us how they created their shirt.

Materials:

1. Project directions and sample
2. Book/novel
3. White T-shirts (These can often be purchased on sale at craft scores for under $3.00 each.)
4. Markers, craft paint, iron-ons, craft glue

* For those who may be unable to obtain art supplies, I gather extra materials that students can take home and return. (Buying these items in August during back-to-school sales is a great way to save money.)

Cost: $$
Prep time: First time, 2 hours. After that, minimal.
Project duration: 3–5 weeks

Home support: Some help may be required, such as a visit to the craft store.

ELL support: Provide directions to parents in the language that is spoken at home.

Alterative: Cut out T-shirts from oversized white construction paper and students can design their T-shirts using crayons or markers. T-shirts can be placed on wire clothes hangers and displayed in the classroom.

PARADE FLOATS

At the time of the Rose Bowl, each student is assigned a state to research. As part of their research report, they must create a shoebox float that represents the geography, people, resources, government, and culture of their state. The float is to be designed to look like those that appear at the Rose Bowl Parade. Students share their floats with the class, and we celebrate by having our own State Float Parade. Since this project requires a lot of craft supplies, it may be done partially in school in collaboration with the art teacher. If your school has a librarian, they will be a great resource to help students gather information for their projects. Note: this project can easily be tweaked to showcase study on countries, continents, cultures, or even people.

Materials:

1. Shoebox
2. Various art supplies, like paper, markers, glue
3. Books, computers/internet for research

Cost: $

Prep time: Minimal. I show students samples of what parade floats look like.

Project duration: 3–4 weeks

Home support: Some home support will be needed.

ELL support: Provide directions to parents in the language that is spoken at home.

SHARK TANK

I love the television show *Shark Tank*, where entrepreneurs pitch their ideas to a group of investors (the "sharks") in hope of forming a partnership. For our Shark Tank, students must think of a problem they face and either design or improve upon an invention or product that will solve the problem. Before beginning the project, we watch an episode of *Shark Tank* and students take notes on details they notice, focusing on what gets the sharks to invest in a product.

By using the NGSS engineering standards (ETS1A, B, and C) as guidelines, students are free to build a prototype, create a drawing, or design a virtual model. Similar to the television show, students come to school ready to pitch their idea to a group of "sharks," so they must use their personal presentation skills to persuade the "sharks" to "invest" in them. I invite four or five guest teachers, staff members, or school administrators to play the role of the sharks. To make it a competition, I give each shark a $100,000 investing budget.

Students follow the following format when completing their project:

1. Generate an idea.
2. Target their target audience.
3. Brainstorm ways the product will be advertised.
4. Determine the cost of making the product.
5. Determine a wholesale and resale price.
6. Decide how much money they will be asking the sharks for and what the money will be used for.
7. Build or design their prototype.
8. Present their idea to the class/group of "sharks"

Materials:

1. Student directions
2. Projector to project students' visuals

Cost: $

Prep time: Minimal.

Project duration: 2–3 weeks

Home support: Some help may be required. Students are encouraged to reuse and recycle items they already have. If the students are going to do the project only in class, I group them in pairs or triads.

Collaboration: This is the perfect project to collaborate with a STEM/STEAM teacher, art teacher, librarian, technology teacher, or parent volunteers.

ELL support: Review key vocabulary with students. Provide examples with visuals.

Long-term projects teach kids many more multicurricular skills than any worksheet will ever do, and easily become classroom traditions that former students look back on and future students anticipate completing.

Working in Hollywood

Living and teaching in Los Angeles, I am often asked if I have ever had celebrities as classroom parents. Yes, I have. Los Angeles is the mecca for celebrity sightings: just this week, I sat behind one of my favorite reality star couples at the movies. When I first moved here, it was definitely a novelty seeing celebrities at restaurants, a coffee shop, or sometimes even at the local grocery store. I am guilty of snapping a photo and sending it off to my friends back home. And as a teacher in LA, it's not uncommon to have a celebrity parent or two at your school.

When I first moved here, a student's parent actually asked me to be on an episode of a reality show they were filming. They wanted a scene of me having a parent-teacher conference. The school wouldn't allow it to be filmed on site, so I had to go to their home to film the scene. As a fan of reality television, it was interesting to see what goes into creating an episode.

The best part was this particular family lived in one of the most elite and private neighborhoods in Los Angeles, Hidden Hills, where people like the Kardashians, Jennifer Lopez, and Justin Bieber have homes. It's so private that I wasn't even allowed to drive my own car into the neighborhood (in fear I would take photos and sell them to the tabloids). Producers of the show sent a driver and escorted me to the home.

The gates of Hidden Hills are like those restricting access to Jurassic Park. Two huge wooden gates open onto one of the most lavish communities in the United States. And here I was, in awe. Then there was a second set of gates. My ID was checked twice. I was so overwhelmed by all of this that I didn't take the time to really look around.

We filmed a scene in which I conducted a parent-teacher conference in their home living room. There's A LOT of work that gets put into filming a five-minute scene. I couldn't believe how many people were there! We did the scene twice because there was feedback from my microphone. Other than that, what you saw was what we filmed. I had been in Los Angeles for less than three months, and I had my fifteen minutes of fame.

A few years later, the singer of my favorite band was a parent in my class. Meeting for the first time was pretty crazy. It was the first day of school. Not only do we as teachers have "first day of school butterflies," but imagine knowing that it's likely you will be meeting one of your idols! As I stood outside the classroom door, greeting new students and their parents, I looked up, and there she was. She was standing right in front of me. Her hand out, shaking my hand, introducing herself to me with her first name (as if I didn't already know). She looked just like she did in photos and was dressed to perfection from head to toe. And over the course of that school year, her son and I formed a close bond. After the school year was over, she extended invitations to see her in concert, and even to her home for birthday parties and barbeques.

Teaching in Hollywood has led to several of these disconcerting moments. A few years ago, I was giving teachers PD on student engagement. That same day, our school administration was offering campus tours to perspective parents. About fifty teachers were sitting in the science lab, listening to me ramble—then I looked up, and a member from a '90s boy band and his beautiful wife were standing in the doorway. They just peeked in and slipped out as quickly as they entered. I literally stopped in the middle of the sentence, completely flabbergasted. When I knew he was gone, I yelled out to my audience of colleagues, "Oh my god, that was . . . " We all laughed (my face was completely flushed), and then we moved on to my next bullet point.

When I worked at the start-up charter school, the level of dedication from the parent body was incredible. In the two years I worked there, the parents of my students were determined to help me in any way possible. The school only employed one custodian, which meant our classrooms were only cleaned once a week. Parents volunteered to come in to clean the classroom after school. And I mean *clean*. Wash the floors, vacuum the carpet, and disinfect the desks. If I needed anything for a lesson, those parents found a way to get it to me. When I left that school, I was just as sad to say goodbye to the parents as I was to my students. Their level of commitment to their children's education was so strong and admirable. Another example of it taking a village.

As teachers, I think it's important that we join and become active members of our school's parent-teacher organization. Whether it's a PTA or a PTO, schools that actively create these forms of parent-teacher collaboration seem to have happier teachers and parents. A parent-teacher team helps build empathy with the school's two largest stakeholders.

In New York, I sat on the executive board of our PTO for seven years. Despite the evening meetings, it's an excellent way to learn about the inner workings of your school community and to be a voice for teachers, too. Our PTO was incredible. They put on event after event for the students, with the parents on that PTO working endlessly to run book fairs, school dances, festivals, and assemblies. The list was truly endless. The PTO also supported the teachers by providing breakfasts and lunches throughout the year, and even giving teachers gift cards at the beginning of each year. In the twelve years I worked at the school in New York, we never had a problem getting teachers or parents to participate in after-hours events. Both parties had similar goals and felt mutual respect.

The PTO even helped organize our holiday staff parties. As someone who enjoys the art of party planning, I took on the role of organizing our annual December holiday party. In addition to my team of colleagues, the parents also helped me. They got to the venue early to help set up, went to local businesses to obtain the prizes that we raffled off, and later, would come and help clean up.

Some of my closest friends are the parents of former students. I understand I am not going to be everyone's cup of tea, and none of us will become friends with every parent who enters our classroom, but those home-to-school connections are a vital part of a blockbuster classroom and create a meaningful community for student growth and support.

Educator Spotlight: Small Notes, Big Changes

In 2013, I moved about four hours from my family and friends to a place where I knew no one. I was also only one of a few teachers of color at my school. The school was made up of predominantly white teachers and students. It was very clear that, even in 2013, I would not have an easy time being accepted as the new kindergarten teacher. A few months into my second year at the school, I knew I needed to do something different to get the parents "on my side" before having parent-teacher conferences and telling a few of them things that would be hard to hear.

I started writing quick little notes in just a few kids' agendas each day. Every day it was a different two or three children. It was a bit time-consuming, but I wanted to let them know their child was having a great day, working hard to persevere, or helping out a friend. These little notes started to receive great feedback. The parents would write back their own little notes. It was one small step in the direction of creating a team of parents who were there for their children and our classroom.

After a while of writing notes, I ran out of ideas of things to say, and instead, got the bright idea to make some small premade notes, print them on colored paper, and put them in an envelope. Every time I saw a child doing something, I would pull out a piece of my premade notepaper and jot down a note. At the end of the day, I would stick the positive notes in their mailboxes. When it was time to pack backpacks, students were surprised to find their notes. Soon, the end of the day became more exciting because they all wanted to see who go "the note" that day. The funniest thing also happened: my students started to notice when other students were doing things that were "noteworthy," and we began praising each other during the day.

That one thought about trying to create a positive home-to-school connection ended up allowing my students to see the good in others, as well. My relationship with my students' parents allowed me to have those tough conversations with them without fear they would become upset. This relationship also opened  them up to being more present. After that year, I continued to make copies of my notes at the beginning of each school year so I could make sure I said at least one positive thing every day to a family about their child.

Keri Brown, kindergarten teacher
@enchantedkindergarden

ACTION!

1. List three ways you can you improve communication with parents.

2. In what ways can you get parents to communicate with you?

3. What's your philosophy on homework? Does your homework philosophy match your school's home-work policy?

4. Are there any units of study or content standards for which you can create a long-term project?

5. Does your school encourage teachers to be part of the parent-teacher organiza-tion? If not, is there another way you can become involved?

CHAPTER NINE

The Swiss Family Robinson

Colleagues

The Swiss Family Robinson got shipwrecked and became isolated on an island. The family had to work together to accomplish their simple goal: survival. They find a way to make the best of what they have, including taking care of each other while undergoing several adventures. Teaching can be a very isolating profession. People might not think so, but most of our days as educators are spent with kids, not adults. We often have to work through our lunches, and our prep periods are busy photocopying, grading papers, or updating Google Classroom. It's too easy to go through an entire day without having an adult conversation.

Our fellow teachers are our codirectors. Our day-to-day tasks are similar and although they take place in different locations and we sometimes address different subjects, we all have the same goal: creating a memorable educational experience for students. Our codirectors don't only include the other teachers we work with, but our entire school staff. These codirectors include paraprofessionals, office staff, the custodial and maintenance crew, school nurses, and school security. Any successful school needs codirectors, because everyone's role is essential.

A few years ago, I visited my friend Alice's school in the Los Angeles area. She is the principal, and immediately upon entering her school, I could tell that this place was bursting with positivity. She introduced me to everyone the same way, and no one was left out or treated differently. People were smiling and greeted me with eye contact and firm handshakes. School culture was something the school took pride in and held people accountable for.

As teachers, we cannot control the school culture, but we can certainly maintain the culture of our classrooms. I teach my students that everyone who enters our classroom space is equally important, that there should be no difference in how we greet and treat the principal from any other school employee or visitor.

I worked at a school that didn't offer the teachers or staff a break room. Not having a faculty room made it very challenging for the school staff to bond and interact in a casual setting. Our only choices were to eat in our classrooms, find a quiet place outside (not easy), or eat in our cars (depressing). A staff room serves a greater purpose than simply being a place for people to each lunch. It provides a place for teachers and staff members to exchange information, commiserate, make connections, and occasionally talk shop with colleagues whom they may not get to see regularly.

I recently visited a friend's school and immediately became envious of their teacher's room. It was filled with beautiful furniture, a television, a book corner, two refrigerators, two microwaves, and several Keurig-style coffee makers. There were houseplants (totally my jam) and beautifully framed photos of the teachers and their families. It was immediately apparent how much the school valued their teaching staff. Being nosy, I asked if all schools in the district have teacher rooms like this. Turns out, no. They all have staff rooms, but *this* was special: their parent-teacher organization did the entire room from floor to ceiling, and it didn't cost the school a penny. Bam—relationships matter.

If there was one piece of advice I'd give new teachers, it would be to get to know the names and roles of everyone who works at your school. One of the first people I had the opportunity to meet and interact with on my first day was the head maintenance person, Jose. Jose is a mastermind. In my opinion, there's nothing he can't do. He is there before school, after school, on the weekend, during vacations. He helps anyone with anything they need, and if he can't do it, he finds someone who can. In addition to eating lunch with my fifth grade team, Jose eats with us, too, so I spend more time with him then I do with many teachers I work with. We as teachers must model for our students that everyone is treated with respect, not just other teachers. My students love Mr. Jose (it's his preference to be called by his first name) and know what a vital member of the school community he is. All relationships matter.

As I mentioned in the introduction, I was hired midyear for my first teaching job, directly out of student teaching. I hadn't even graduated from college or finished student teaching. I was twenty-two years old and had no experience running my own classroom. I knew no kids, or any parents. But Nellie Maldanado, one of the school secretaries, got me through those first hard months of teaching. I will never forget Nellie's kindness. We teachers all know the secretaries run the school, and they know everything and everyone. If I have a second piece advice for anyone reading this book, it's to be nice to your school secretaries.

Nellie didn't know me from a hole in the wall, but I think she appreciated my smile and genuine gratitude. Maybe she looked at me as a son-like figure, but without her help, my first six months of teaching would have been much harder. Nellie looked out for me and always answered my (ridiculous) questions with a smile. The following fall, I was hired for a tenure-track position at another building in the district, and over the years, Nellie and I lost touch, but I remember her kindness often.

Open Your Classroom Door

So many books will tell us to shut our classroom door and do our own thing. Yes, that may be the easy thing to do. But living within four walls of your classroom is lonely. Sometimes, we need to close the door and keep our focus, but it's also crucial that we open up and invite people into our space. Not everyone may want to come in, but seek out the people who do.

INVITING PEOPLE INTO YOUR SPACE:

- Host a book club.
- Plan lessons together.
- Team-teach a lesson.
- Host and participate in virtual PD.
- Organize a lesson study.

Two or three times a year, I host and facilitate a book club before school. We meet once a week, and I serve coffee, have breakfast desserts, and play relaxing music in the background. This book club is the perfect way to let people into my space and get the chance to collaborate with colleagues I wouldn't often see.

It's a pity that, generally, the school day is not designed for cross-collaboration. Faculty meetings are often held at the end of the day when people are exhausted and carrying emotional baggage from their day. Prep periods are usually not aligned with other teachers', and in my experience, when they are, administrators will use them to hold parent meetings or mandatory, noncollaborative PD.

So how can we as teachers break the system, tweak it, find a way to beat it?

Collaboration between colleagues is a must for a school to be successful. It improves and streamlines the curriculum, aligns student and teacher expectations, and benefits the school culture. Horizontal and vertical collaboration are vital ingredients in a successful school. Administrators need to give teachers time to plan and review the curriculum together.

One of my favorite ways to collaborate with colleagues is through a lesson study. A lesson study is when a group (usually a triad of three teachers who teach the same content) works together to design and execute a lesson. Each person contributes to planning the lesson, which is then taught by each person in the group and observed by the others. The observers are not critiquing the teacher executing the lesson, but instead focus on the students and student outcomes. After the lesson has been taught, the lesson study group meets to debrief. Then, the lesson is refined, and the process is repeated until each member has taught the lesson.

Sample Lesson Study: Lesson Plan

INTRODUCTION

In this section:

1. Briefly describe the lesson.
2. List the members of your lesson study team.

BACKGROUND CONTEXT

In this section:

- Explain the rationale for selecting the topic (e.g., it's a particularly difficult topic for students; it's a new area of the curriculum.)

ESSENTIAL QUESTIONS

Essential questions are designed to encourage further inquiry into a particular subject. They're intended to spark a conversation about the subject rather than simply provide a factual answer to the question. For example, rather than asking students what the three branches of government are, an essential question would ask, "What would prevent the US government from overstepping its authority?"

ESSENTIAL QUESTIONS:

- Are open-ended and don't have a single, final, and correct answer.
- Are thought-provoking and intellectually engaging; they also promote discussion and debate.
- Call for higher-order thinking, such as analysis, inference, evaluation, and prediction: they can't be answered effectively by recall alone.

LESSON DESIGN

Grade level: What grade are the students in?

Learning objectives: What are the objectives of your lesson?

Standards: What standard(s) does the lesson teach?

Materials and resources: List the materials and resources students will be using.

Lesson structure: How is the lesson organized? Include the amount of time that will be spent with direct instruction, independent practice, group/partner work, and the closure.

Assessment: How will students be assessed?

ANALYSIS OF THE LESSON

In this section:

1. Describe the types of evidence of student learning you collected, including:
   - observations of student learning and thinking during the lesson;

- evaluation of student learning before and/or after the lesson.

2. Summarize the results in terms of what students learned (based on any pre- and post-lesson evidence) and how they learned or did not learn what was taught (based on observational evidence from the lesson).

3. Explain the results. Based on the evidence, how did the lesson support (and not support) achievement of the learning goals? Explain other "interesting" findings, even if they are not directly related to the lesson goals. Discuss the significance of the results and what they mean for improving the lesson.

REFLECTION

In this section:

1. Tell the reader what you have learned from the lesson study and how it has affected your classroom instruction and/or pedagogical thinking. Cite specific examples to illustrate changes in your practices or thinking after collaborating with your team members.

SOME PROMPTS

1. Why did you become involved in lesson study? What are your teaching-improvement goals?

2. Discuss specific insights about student learning that came out of the lesson study.

3. Discuss ways your teaching has changed or begun to change in terms of class planning, goal setting, classroom practices, assessment of student learning, use of assessment to improve teaching and learning, and your understanding of how students learn the subject you teach.

4. How has collaboration helped meet school-wide, grade-level, or curriculum goals?

If your school isn't able to conduct a lesson study, try team-teaching a lesson with another teacher. Recently, I decided to give this a try during my Dessert Cafe lesson simulation, when I turn my classroom into a cafe and students order from a menu. Students then must calculate the tax and tip using our previous math lesson on percentages. As something new, I invited the other fifth-grade math teacher in to team-teach the lesson with me.

So, one Friday, we combined classes and created Kevin and Mary's Delicious Dessert Cafe. The kids LOVED it, and so did Mary. So not only did we have fun, we learned from each other. She put a little bit of herself into the lesson, I put a little bit of myself into the lesson, and we have a memory that we will talk about at our retirement party. It also modeled what real-world collaboration looks like.

In her book *Educational Eye Exam*, Alicia Ray writes about the importance of sharing and how we as educators should be tapping into each other's strengths. A great way to do this is by creating a professional learning community (PLC). A PLC is a type of PD in which

teachers join a team of others who share ideas to enhance their teaching practice. Throughout my career, I have participated in several PLCs and have walked away with new ideas that I was able to implement in my classroom.

Ideally, the PLC works on the bones of a lesson, with different educators adding ideas to improve student learning. I've also participated in PLCs where the group collaborates to study fresh ideas in education, review school data, implement best practices, and attend professional development.

Educator Spotlight:
A Star Is Born . . . When We Collaborate

As an administrator, creating a culture of collaboration on a campus is extremely important, but in the world of education, collaboration can be a difficult task. Often, teachers have an opportunity to work with their content team in small increments without the chance to branch out beyond their subject matter. As I gathered data in classrooms and had conversations with my staff, it was evident that the teachers were facilitating many creative lessons, implementing technology applications, and providing engaging strategies in their classrooms. The problem was that no one knew the incredible strategies occurring in one another's classrooms. One teacher was a magician at classroom management, and another was a rock star at assessments. However, neither teacher knew the strengths of their colleagues.

I met with the campus leadership team to combat the lack of collaboration and brainstorm new ideas. We created a teacher-led professional development (PD) program called the "Creative Corner." The idea was that, once a month, we would have a voluntary PD session after school to share a classroom strategy or innovative technique. The goal was to have a teacher from our campus or a district leader share tips and tricks on how to deliver the best instructional practices. The leadership team agreed that the teachers needed more tools to increase engagement, provide immediate assessment feedback, and enhance student collaboration.

After the leadership meeting, we communicated to the staff about the program. Each month on the third Wednesday of the month, we conducted a voluntary Creative Corner PD session and usually saw a third of the staff attend each session. The Creative Corner program gave our teachers a safe space to learn from their peers, ask questions, and explore new classroom techniques. Teachers shared and discussed a variety of tools, such as Flipgrid, Google applications, Chrome extensions, voice to text, and assessment programs.

The program received a lot of positive feedback from the staff, and the teachers appreciated that it empowered every educator in the building. Each campus has so many wonderful teachers with engaging and creative ideas. As leaders, it is our job to find opportunities for our teachers to work together and learn the amazing techniques occurring in each classroom. Teaching is a difficult job, and we don't need to do it alone. As an educational community, we have to help each other, find new solutions, and allow everyone to be a classroom star.

Joshua Stamper, administrator, author of *Aspire to Lead*, podcast host, and podcast network manager for the Teach Better team
@joshua_stamper

IDEAS FOR PLC FOCUS TOPICS:

1. STEM/STEAM
2. Social-emotional learning

3. Mentoring
4. Review of school novels to ensure students are exposed to a variety of diverse characters, settings, authors, illustrators, and themes
5. Book study
6. Examining school data

Another thing our school staff did was to invite different grade-level teachers to host breakfast in the faculty room each month. The monthly breakfast included each member of that grade-level group bringing in various items, such as bagels, muffins, juice, and coffee. It wasn't a massive party, but it was nice to know that we had something to look forward to on the last Friday of each month. We also began creating monthly happy hours, which became ingrained into our calendar. While it was optional, we always had a large group of teachers and staff members stop by for a drink and to celebrate another month closer to summer vacation.

Another fun bonding event was to play the lottery together. One of our teachers would collect five or ten dollars from each teacher (entirely optional) and buy as many lottery tickets as possible. Sadly, we never won big, but again, it created moments to look forward to.

When I was working at a start-up school, teachers were given release days to plan with their team members and also to complete report cards. The principal encouraged us to work off-campus, at someone's home or at a local coffee shop. This offered us an entire day to plan for long-term projects and collaborate on things like creating grading rubrics. I wish more schools offered this relatively easy and inexpensive way to help teachers collaborate.

Building empathy with colleagues isn't always easy, though. Everyone (I am guilty of this, too) thinks their job is more demanding and that everyone else has it easier. Many years ago, back in New York, my principal wanted the staff to build empathy toward each other. At a faculty meeting, he announced that all teachers would be switching roles for a day. Kindergarten teachers would teach sixth grade, PE teachers would teach art, music teachers would teach technology, and so on.

I was not a happy camper. I had to teach first grade for the day, and I was terrified! The day before the switch, we were given release time to collaborate with the teacher we would be switching with. It turned out that the first grade teacher I was switching with was just as nervous as me. We went over our plans together and discussed our schedules and student information. The next day, I taught first grade for the first and only time. It was fun, and I am glad I had the experience, but I wouldn't do that every day! However, what an excellent exercise for building empathy.

One of my all-time favorite things I helped create and organize is called Crazy Sports Night. Every constituent of our school collaborated for an all-out battle of crazy sporting events between the four elementary schools in our district. *Everyone* participated, including classroom teachers, specialists, administrators, members of the board of education, and even our superintendent. Each year, it was standing room only. We initially held the event at our elementary building, but

after a while, the elementary gymnasium was not big enough to hold the number of parents and kids who wanted to attend.

So, we moved the event to the massive junior-senior high gymnasium and actually had to lock people out of the building because we were at maximum capacity. What made this special is that everyone was there for the same reason: to *win*! Just kidding—we were there to have fun. I'll never forget how an entire school system came together on a Friday night to battle each other in things like tug-of-war, obstacle courses, and a plethora of other ridiculous games in front of a thousand students and their parents. The PTA even sold merchandise and food in the lobby. This was a bonding activity and became a huge fundraiser for the school. It does take a village.

When the games were over and the winning school had been crowned, the competitors would meet at a local restaurant and share drinks and laughs. Yes, Crazy Sports Night was silly—but at heart it was all about building bonds and creating memories. Relationships matter.

If you have ever or will ever work with me, you will know how much the Ron Clark Academy has impacted my career. The thing about going to RCA is that you spend time in real classrooms, getting to see different teachers teach real lessons to real kids. I have learned so much by observing other teachers teach and kids learn; the bonus there is that you're getting to observe master teachers in their natural habitat. I've taken more away from my ten visits to RCA than from all the teaching conferences I have ever attended combined.

As much as I love visiting RCA, you don't need to go to RCA to see other teachers. I truly believe that some of the best professional development lies in our own school's classrooms. As teachers, we must prioritize reaching out from our own classroom islands to visit and spend time in our colleagues' classrooms.

Educator Spotlight:
Being the Difference

On a bone-chilling Monday morning one January, I stood outside the front doors of my school welcoming in the students for another great week of learning. As principal, it was my duty to be present to greet my school community each day. Like many mornings, one of my student's grandparents walked up to the front door with her grandchild. With a slow Southern drawl and a wry smile, she said to me, "Only reason I'mma wake up this early each day is to see what suit you be wearin'."

I believe in the power of positivity. I believe in the ability we hold as humans to make each other smile, laugh, and find joy. I believe in the moments we can create for others through simple acts. For me, my eclectic suit collection has become an agent for others to find happiness, even on a bitter cold Monday morning. My ever-growing collection has turned into a way for me to connect with people through conversation and laughter.

Yes, these suits look ridiculous. Walking around in tiger print, smiley-face emojis, or Tetris blocks is not exactly what you would expect from a school leader. But for over a decade, I have experienced the joy and smiles on people's faces as they see them, and for me that makes it all worth it. I don't share this to convince you to buy eccentric suits, but rather to find your moments of joy each day. And when possible, create those moments for others. Imagine what your school hallways would feel like if individuals aimed to put smiles on each other's faces. A simple hello, a compliment, or an inquiry into how your day is going are simple things that go a long way, especially for those who need it most. You can make the difference in someone's life.

A few years after the student's grandma told me that my suits encouraged her to wake up early each morning, I learned that she had cancer. She died shortly thereafter. I went to the funeral, where her granddaughter told me that her grandma had known she had cancer the entire time she was dropping her off

at school. She said that waking up in the morning was truly a struggle, but those suits helped her smile through all of the pain. So anytime someone laughs or smiles upon seeing my suits, I know that I am doing what I set out to do.

Adam Dovico, school administrator
@adamdovico

ACTION!

1. Create a list of people in your school who make a difference.

2. How can you open your classroom door and collaborate with others?

3. How might you organize a lesson study with your colleagues?

4. Identify classroom teachers or specialists whom you could team-teach a lesson with.

5. How can you set up a PLC at your school? What topic(s) would you want to focus on?

6. Do teachers in your school empathize with each other? If not, what can be done to create that culture?

CHAPTER TEN

Mission Impossible

Administrators

I n the 1996 thriller *Mission Impossible*, US government operative
Ethan Hunt must go on what seems to be an impossible task that
involves retrieving a highly classified computer file in order to prove
his innocence. School administrators are often given endless tasks that
at times feel impossible.

Teachers choose to leave the classroom to become school administrators for a broad array of reasons: many want to use their leadership abilities to make change, others want to grow professionally, and
possibly some do it for an increase in pay. But whatever the reason
or combination of reasons, bless them, because school administrators
have challenging jobs.

School administrators are often stuck in between a rock and a hard
place. As teachers, we can usually make most people happy. Generally,
if our students are happy, their parents are happy. If parents are happy,
our administrators are happy. But how about administrators? Generally
speaking, they are always dealing with someone who has a problem or
complaint—and that's on top of handling their own work!

For the last six years, I have been a member of my school's
administrative team as the coordinator for K–6 curriculum and

instruction. Since I have never wanted to be a principal, but I love curriculum, this was a great opportunity for me to see into the world of school administration.

Originally, this unique role was designed for me to work alongside the principals of the lower and upper school campuses in the area of curriculum development and improving and implementing new instructional practices. It didn't take me long to learn that an administrative position covers much more than what's listed in the job description.

TIPS for Teachers to Build Relationships with Their Administrators

- Welcome school leaders into your classrooms, not to just observe but to engage with students, be guest readers, help teach a lesson, or just play a game.
- Include your school leaders in celebrations like happy hours and holiday parties.
- Avoid complaining via email. Connect in person and focus on creating constructive solutions.
- Seek out opportunities to help create school schedules, review curriculum, and write school policies.
- Attend PD with school leaders.

As a member of an administrative team, every meeting I attended was jam-packed. Time was precious. There was so much to do and never enough time to get it all done. I don't know if, as a teacher, I ever imagined how much goes on behind the scenes of a school at any given moment. Plus, in this overpacked schedule, everyone had their own priorities and things that needed to be shared.

After becoming a twelve-month employee, I no longer had summers off. I realized just how precious those two summer months are. It's when we as teachers are able to reflect, rejuvenate, and rekindle our passions. It's time that we can spend with family and friends, enjoying hobbies, and indulging in some professional development as we begin to prepare for the new year.

There are several accomplishments I am proud of from my time as a school administrator. My first task was to write a new academic scope and sequence. During that first summer as the curriculum and instructional coordinator, and with the help of my colleague Lauren, I gathered all the curricula teachers were using and documented what was being done at each grade level. My second summer was spent on creating a K–5 skills report card. This was a massive task only accomplished with the help and collaboration of the teaching staff. We spent months fine-tuning the standards and skill-based report card, and it was a huge success.

Other things I enjoyed accomplishing were rolling out a K–5 reading program, aligning reading and math benchmarking, updating our social studies curriculum, and facilitating and organizing PD on student engagement and best teaching practices.

Sadly, that all came to a halt in the spring of 2020. Since then, we haven't had any advancements in curriculum or in-person instruction. I completely understand that Covid-19 threw a wrench into teaching, but schools were not closed, only the *buildings* were. Education needed to continue, and we had to be innovative.

Recently, I have decided to pause my role as curriculum coordinator and focus my time and energy back on teaching, with time for self-care. I'm very happy being a teacher, but I have a lot of empathy for school leaders. It takes a very special person to be a good leader.

I have had the privilege of working with some incredible administrators throughout my years of teaching, and without them, I would not be where I am today. The one thing all of these school leaders have in common is that they were once classroom teachers. I can't fathom the benefit of schools having leaders who have not been teachers. People who do not have classroom experience are not positioned to make decisions about how classrooms are managed.

Successful school leaders do not simply need classroom experience; they need to be *in* the classrooms they are in charge of. Collaboration cannot just happen between teachers; it also needs to happen between teachers and administrators. A good administrator will find time to get into classrooms (and not just for observing teachers). I would not have survived my first year of teaching if it were not for my principal. He was also new, young, and wasn't afraid of implementing change. He spent a lot his first year in classrooms. Making observations of who was doing what, who was good at what, and what could be done to improve the school. And he had the backs of good teachers.

If I could require administrators to read any book, I would choose Ron Clark's *Move Your Bus*. Comparing employees to runners, joggers, walkers, riders, and drivers, he explains ways to accelerate success in the workplace. Good leaders, he says, need to take care of their runners and joggers, and sometimes it's necessary to kick off people who aren't pulling their weight. I wish more administrators understood the concept that a school can only be as strong as its weakest members. Ron gives specific, actionable advice on how to speed up your bus, and thereby change the culture of a school in ways that will help everyone be their best.

One year, I was teaching a student who was experiencing a lot of difficulty in school. He was demonstrating behavior challenges as well as earning low grades. Toward the end of the year, his parents wanted my head on a silver platter. I later discovered that there was a lot happening at home, and I was the person they were releasing their anger on. After this student's third report card and parent-teacher conference, the parents wanted their son removed from my classroom. Literally taken out and placed in another teacher's class for the last seven or eight weeks of school. I remember being called into the principal's office that day . . . I knew right away that something wasn't right.

Rather than yelling or interrogating me, the principal calmly explained to me what the parents had requested and informed me that he'd told the parents he would not be removing the student from my class. He also said that I had done nothing wrong—but that I needed to make the next seven weeks of this student's life in school wonderful. He told me to do whatever I needed to do to make him feel happy and productive. The other things that were happening at home I had no control over. The only thing I could control was that this student felt safe and happy at school.

The only reason my principal (who, again, was just as new to the school as I was) was able to support me and stand up to those parents was because he knew me, he knew how I taught, and what was (and wasn't) happening in my classroom. He was a normal fixture in the classroom. He didn't only come into my classroom to observe me, but it was his normal behavior to nonchalantly walk in and out of the class-rooms. To come in as a guest reader, teach a lesson, or simply partici-pate in the shenanigans of the day. There was a legitimate relationship there. Because of that, he was without a doubt able to tell the parents of that child that it was in his best interest to stay in my classroom.

Ten Things that Make a Great School Leader (and Appreciative Teachers)

1. Set and keep realistic expectations and timelines for teachers, such as when rolling out new curriculum.
2. Prioritize spending time in classrooms.
3. Provide teachers with constructive feedback and ideas to help them reach their goals.
4. Protect teachers from difficult parents.
5. Be honest and transparent. It's okay to say no or that you do not have an answer right now.
6. Never gossip about other teachers.
7. Listen to teachers and avoid becoming defensive when teachers vent to you.
8. Normalize the teacher workday. Understand that teachers are not on call twenty-four hours a day, seven

---

days a week. Avoid sending teachers emails outside the normal workday hours, and never on weekends. Support your staff when they need to use their contracted sick days and personal time.

9. Use email to relay information rather than holding meetings.

10. Move staff meetings to the morning, when teachers' minds are less cluttered. Make staff meetings productive and collaborative.

Collaborating with administrators might not always be easy, but it's certainly possible. Teachers have to stop approaching dialogues with administrators with an "us against them" mindset. We need to be responsible for including them and keeping our classroom doors open for them to enter. Whenever I do one of my room simulations, I always try to invite administrators in. One, it's beneficial for me because they get to see students fully engaged in some pretty cool academic content. Second, it's fun for them. Most of the good administrators I know want to be in your classroom, but don't want to make you feel uncomfortable. But they genuinely want to see our students learning, so I highly encourage you to invite them in. It's a game changer.

I also don't invite administrators in simply to observe. I give them roles, and I prep them ahead of time. I want them to be just as actively engaged in the lessons as my students and I are. Whether they are reading a book or joining us in one of our room simulations, they're a part of it.

Teachers cannot be the only ones asking administrators to collaborate; our administrators should also do their part in reaching out to teachers. Every school has their natural leaders, those teachers whom administrators are always inviting to be on various committees. But good administrators should not only rely on those teachers who always volunteer. They must find ways to pull everyone into being an active member of their school community—or at least try to. In general, though, people want to be invited to be heard. People who feel as if they are listened to, that their opinion matters, will work harder. Good administrators create time to meet with teachers to collaborate, find ways to support new ideas, and encourage others to get on board (or get off the ship). Good administrators will also take care of their best teachers.

Educator Spotlight:
Leadership for Student Learning

Yousuf Karsh says to "look and think before opening the shutter. The heart and mind are the true lens of the camera." In January 2017, I became the principal of Meadow Woods Elementary. I had to quickly develop my vision. A photograph captures a specific moment in time. When would I open my shutter, and which lens would I need? How could I empower the students who were currently out of focus? My time at Meadow Woods would be composed of the moments I chose to capture. I needed to be observant, clear, and patient to ensure my vision would fully come to life to meet the current needs of the community. Equity for all students was the framing principle.

My first days were spent overseeing the construction of a new school while trying to manage numerous discipline concerns and low family engagement. Most notably, I observed parts of a student body, a faculty, and a community that were feeling disconnected during the renovation of their campus. I implemented culturally responsive strategies to engage the predominantly Hispanic community as their first-ever Spanish-speaking principal. Realizing that many families carried trauma, I started my journey toward helping all families feel connected. When Hurricane Maria devastated Puerto Rico, it expedited my mission to be a trauma-informed school. While our school became home to forty-two families seeking refuge, I prioritized the development of our Family Resource Center. It has been recognized by the news, district, and the Department of Education's 2019–2020 Family and Community Involvement Award.

I had to ensure my staff concentrated on the instructional needs of all subgroups, so I provided strategic professional development and equipped staff with strategies to design calm, inviting classrooms. I continued to recognize teachers for their innovation and creativity and celebrated small wins. My teachers took risks that resulted in high-caliber instruction and engagement as they transformed their classrooms into atmospheres that appealed to the senses and broke the barriers of traditional instruction. My investment in human capital showed in staff morale, but also in a 7 percent increase in ELA learning gains, 13 percent increase in math learning gains, 11 percent in ELA lowest 25 percent, and 17 percent in math lowest 25 percent, from 2017–2018 to 2018–2019.

As my staff embraced trauma-informed practices, we saw increased academic performance, while referrals declined from 92 (2016–2017) to 59 (2019–2020) with a 37 percent increase in student enrollment. In one year, physical behaviors decreased from 115 to 34 incidents, emotional behaviors decreased from 165 to 145 incidents, and social behaviors decreased from 85 to 58 incidents.

In three years of my leadership, several staff members have become building leaders, including a principal, assistant princi-

pals, and other leaders within the district. They trusted me to grow their strengths and provide honest feedback to help improve their pedagogy. As a principal, I know that I have many moments left to capture, using my heart and mind.

Aleli Vazquez, school administrator

A powerful way for administrators, school staff, and parents to collaborate is to create a building leadership team (BLT). This is a team that meets monthly to discuss school-level issues, goals, and activities. Unlike being placed on a committee, all are welcome, and there's no commitment to attend every meeting. I have found these beneficial to bringing together people who may not necessarily collaborate. Someone (usually the principal) acts as organizer, someone else creates an agenda, and a third person keeps minutes. These meetings are usually informal, last for thirty minutes, and take place before school when people are fresh. And because BLT meetings are open to all, they build positive school culture.

TIPS for Building Administrators Teacher Relationships

- Celebrate, uplift, and support your best teachers. They are the ones who will go above and beyond the call of duty for you, their students, and the school community.
- Stop asking teachers to work for free. Compensate them for joining committees, attending meetings, and working outside of contractual hours. If compensation can't be monetary, then think outside of the box.
- Leave positive notes. I have saved every note an administrator has left me after visiting my classroom. Something as small as a "nice job" or "thank you" on a Post-it note goes a long way.
- Share positive feedback you receive from parents. Forward teachers positive emails you receive from parents.
- When you need to meet with teachers, let them know why. It can ruin a teacher's entire day when you send an email saying, "Stop by my office when you have a chance."

The last principal I had in New York was an amazing colleague. I remember meeting Sal for the first time days after he was approved by the BOE to become the new principal of our elementary school. Another teacher and I had been asked to give him a tour of the school and introduce him to everyone. He was close to my age, fresh, and full of enthusiasm. I instantly knew I would like working with him. Sal was also a former classroom teacher (as I think all administrators should be). Over the time I got to work with Sal, he was always up for collaborating. He was a frequent visitor to our classroom and participated in all of our school events. He knew the students' names, and his office door was always open.

Once, Sal even joined a group of teachers I was facilitating a PLC with on a trip down to the Ron Clark Academy in Atlanta, Georgia. He spent two days learning hands-on with our teacher PLC. He was managing a school with one thousand students, but Sal made time to collaborate and bond with his teachers. When we returned, it was easier for our core team of teachers to implement some of the strategies school-wide that we had learned at RCA. Relationships matter.

And most of all, teachers, be kind to your school leaders and admins. Their job is (almost) impossible.

Educator Spotlight:
Don't Be a Lonely Leader

I almost left my job because I was lonely and didn't feel connected to my colleagues. It wasn't their fault; we just had different visions of what the position could and should look like.

It's been twelve years since I had that dreadful feeling when I almost quit my principalship, and I've vowed never to experience it again and to help as many school leaders as I can get connected and build relationships with one another.

If you're a school leader and you're on an educator island in 2022, it's completely up to you.

You're better when you're connected with other leaders in your county, your state, across the country, and all over the world.

My wife was actually the one who encouraged me to stop being a stalker on social media and put myself out there to connect with, learn from, and grow alongside others. And that's exactly what I did.

Go to your favorite social media platform and just search your job title. You're going to find thousands of other people just like you, doing the same exact work in different locations around the world. Give yourself a three-month runway, and for those three months, follow twenty-five other new-to-you school leaders every week. That's exactly where I started more than a dozen years ago.

Engage with them. Learn from them. Reach out to them. Connect with them. Ask questions of them. And add value to them. Because your ideas are important and will add value to the profession.

And then, once you start building that network, you'll start feeling less alone, you'll start collaborating around different ideas, and the work and the problems and everything else will start to feel just a little bit lighter.

Don't be a lonely leader; you deserve to be connected. Connect with me, and I'll be on your team. I believe in you, and I know you can do it.

Adam Welcome, international keynote speaker, author, podcaster, and former elementary school principal
@mradamwelcome

ACTION!

1. How does your school encourage collaboration between teachers/staff and administrators? How could it be improved?

2. In what ways could you become involved in your school decision-making?

3. Would it be possible to create a BLT in your school? If so, create a list of people you would want to have participate. What topics would you want to discuss?

4. What kinds of things would make you as a teacher or an administrator feel appreciated and respected?

The Mask

Lessons from a Pandemic

A t first, Jim Carrey's 1994 comedy *The Mask* may appear to have nothing to do with what teachers went through during the first two years of the global coronavirus pandemic. If you have seen the film, you may remember that when Carrey's timid character puts on the mask, it turns him into a superhero. While we didn't lose all of our inhibitions and become bank robbers like his character, in March 2020, we put on masks and became superheroes.

On Tuesday, March 10, 2020 at 10:00 a.m., I was summoned out of teaching math to the conference room. I sat at a table with school administrators and the school board president. I was briefed that "things"—meaning the world, including schools in Los Angeles—may begin to shut down due to the coronavirus. I, not an alarmist, couldn't believe what I was hearing. Shut *school* down? Why? This was not making any sense. I blurted out that "things like this do not happen in the United States." Boy, was I wrong!

Twelve or so of us sat in that room for well over an hour discussing all the what-ifs. We were texting leaders of other schools in the area to learn about their plans, as no one wanted to be the first school to shut down. The news was streaming, and incoming reports asserted that a complete shutdown was imminent. We decided to hold an after-school meeting with teachers to begin discussing the contingencies and plan for possibly moving our instruction from in-person to online.

That afternoon, our director of technology made sure all teachers had Zoom accounts. The school was already using Google Classroom and an app called Seesaw. We had this, right? Spring break was on the horizon, and, for sure, this would be over in a month and we would be back to "normal."

That night, the news reported a shortage of toilet paper. Wednesday morning, before work, I stopped at the grocery store. What I saw looked like a scene out of an apocalyptic Hollywood movie. I was witnessing fellow customers at my local grocery store tearing open boxes and clearing off shelves with whatever was in reach. Lines went from the checkout counter in the front of the store all the way to the back wall. The anxiety was palpable.

Students left school on Thursday in hope of returning to school on Monday, so school was closed on Friday to prepare and train teachers on processes if we needed to complete in-person instruction. We used Wednesday and Thursday to prepare kids for the possibility of the school closing and reviewing logins for websites, digital citizenship expectations, and how to hand in work electronically.

Teachers also sent students home with all of their workbooks, textbooks, and hard copies of materials they could use to prevent excessive screen time. Our younger grades would be using Seesaw as the primary communication tool between teachers and their students, while the upper grades would use Google Classroom. We were fortunate in being somewhat ready for distance learning, since students and teachers already used these two platforms daily. Our librarian also made sure every student went home with a public library card (some of them brand-new). They knew that, while the libraries might close, there is tons of digital content students can access via their cards.

Our school had a contingency plan in place for circumstances that might cause the school to shut down for an extended period (fire,

earthquakes, etc.). We had a task team review the plan and tweak it before presenting it to the faculty. On Friday, our technology teacher reviewed technology procedures and gave additional training on platforms like the Google Suite and Zoom. Most of the day was dedicated to planning out two weeks of curriculum.

On Monday, our staff was able to come to campus (or work from home) to prepare rolling out Tuesday's lessons. This was a time for our staff and students to learn and grow at an exponential rate. Could we do it?

I was confident that my fifth graders were ready for the challenge. But was I? To be honest, after only two days, I already missed them. I wasn't able to give them a proper goodbye. My fingers were crossed that we would return to school right after spring break.

It took a year for school to reopen.

I returned to campus in March of 2021. There, student desks were placed six feet apart and surrounded with Plexiglas. We were all wearing masks, and several fans were going to circulate the air.

This was not business as usual.

But kids are resilient. They came to school, and we all quickly adapted to the new way of teaching and learning.

Educator Spotlight:
Finding the Good, and Shouting It Out

In my post-pandemic classroom, I implemented a few small changes that I hope have lasting value. One of the changes this year is a quick five-minute morning activity called "Some Good News."

At the beginning of the Covid-19 pandemic, John Krasinski launched his *Some Good News* show to highlight, among all the lockdowns and dark times, some positive, inspiring anecdotes! In this same vein, every moment of my students' daily lives isn't always positive, and students may not always see their day as "good"—but there is good in each day! And I want to celebrate that each morning and start them off on a positive note.

After our basic morning routine and attendance, I loudly, and rather dramatically, announce: "And now it's time for . . . " And my students shout back: "SOME! GOOD! NEWS!" At that point, hands go up and anyone and everyone can share (in one or two sentences) what is good in their life at that moment!

Sometimes it's as simple as "It's Friday!" or "I ate waffles this morning!" Other times, they share about winning soccer games, losing basketball games but playing well, getting their first hit in a baseball game, having their normally grumpy hamster come out willingly for a visit, or petting a puppy while out on a walk the afternoon before. Almost everyone in my class always has something to share!

 The whole activity takes only minutes (typically less than five for us), but what I learn during this time is truly invaluable. Relationships. Positive interactions. Openness. Communication. All of these are key to building a classroom culture where students feel valued and comfortable.

Megan Clappin, fifth grade teacher
@all.about.the.abcs

Yet again, we were pivoting. As teachers and students continued testing positive with Covid-19, we moved to hybrid teaching. Some kids in schools, some kids at home: this was probably the most challenging thing teachers faced during the pandemic. Teaching kids in-person and via Zoom simultaneously was extremely demanding and could be frustrating. One day, I forgot to tell my virtual students that I was taking my in-person students outside for a walk. When the online students signed onto Zoom, no one was in the classroom, and parents were calling the school asking what was going on. I wanted to cry out of embarrassment.

Teaching virtually forced me to learn. I realized I'd become a little complacent with the status quo and now discovered that my students' technological abilities and knowledge had surpassed mine. In a matter of days, I had to learn how to use new technology to do my job. For example, something as simple as giving quizzes using Google Forms was a whole learning curve. However, these tools have saved me endless hours grading paper assignments. As with many teachers around the world, websites and apps I never knew existed are now permanently part of my post-Covid-19 classroom. Blended learning is here to stay.

Many of us also learned just how important those relationships with our students are. I never in a million years would have survived the first two months of the pandemic without having those bonds and classroom traditions established with my students, and I looked forward to Zooming with them. We continued those classroom traditions, holding our morning meetings and adding in afternoon closing circles. I also had to learn to push my creativity. I had to be innovative because I wasn't about to let a virus impact my students' learning.

Student Voice:
Virtual Changes, Same Connections

One day in March 2020, Mr. Butler told us we would have to go home because of Covid-19. Everyone thought we'd be back in a month or two, but that month turned into eleven months. Before Zoom started, Mr. Butler made every day exciting, even Mondays. Before we all headed to the field for PE in the morning, we had a fun mini talk show. Mr. Butler had a student guest and asked them about their weekend or day prior, and they'd talk about it. Then we'd talk about a journal-entry prompt. Something like, "What's your favorite candy?" or "If you could travel anywhere, where would you go?" This was always a great way to start off the day because it made us laugh and learn more about each other. Even though we were in virtual fifth grade for only four months, we could still have the talk show, and we made a lot of memories. Mr. Butler made that time special. He came to our homes and gave us packages (from a distance) to grow our own plants. It was nice to see him. Mr. Butler made virtual school a positive experience for me because he always found ways to make it great and something I'll always remember.

Ellis, class of 2020

After spring break of 2020, we realized that we wouldn't be going back to school anytime soon. Los Angeles was shut down. I remember walking down Ventura Boulevard without seeing a car. I could have walked down the middle of the road for the entire sixty-minute walk and never seen a moving vehicle. It was spooky.

Over that break, I was depressed. There was nowhere to go, no one see, and not much joy in participating in virtual game nights with friends. I worried about my father, who was on the East Coast, not knowing when we could see each other again.

The novelty of virtual school would be wearing off quickly. I missed my students.

It was time to spice things up. Each spring, I plant seeds with my students, who know I love gardening. We usually plant tomatoes, cucumbers, lettuce, marigolds, and sunflowers. I was not giving up on that tradition this year.

I ordered everything from Amazon: the seeds, the soil, little pots, everything students would need to grow an edible garden at home. I packaged everything together and wrote each student a little note. Then, I got planning.

My students live all over Los Angeles in a fifteen-mile radius of our school, stretching across the San Fernando Valley, to Santa Monica, and through the Hollywood Hills. Even without traffic, this would be a trek. I emailed all of the parents and told them I wanted to do a drive-by hello. Following strict Covid-19 health protocols, I would come to their house, deliver their care package and hopefully get to say hello to them (from a distance). Every parent was in, and we picked the date (this was over spring break, so it didn't interfere with school). Then, I mapped it all out and sent parents a schedule. I would begin at 8:00 a.m. and go until 5:00 p.m., making a five-minute stop at each house. The plan was that when I left one house, those parents would text the next family that I was on the way.

I honestly thought I would arrive, drop off the bag, say hello, maybe take a photo and leave. I didn't expect banners, signs, balloons, handmade cards (my favorite), and gifts. I needed this. My teacher's heart had been broken, and seeing all of this instantly made me feel better. Parents handed me bottles of wine, muffins, fresh-picked oranges and lemons, and even dinner! This was what it was all about. Relationships matter.

A few weeks later, I received a direct message from someone claiming to be a producer from *The Kelly Clarkson Show*, saying they'd seen photos of me delivering care packages to my students over spring break during quarantine. I almost didn't respond, but I was curious. The producer asked me to email him a two-minute video explaining what I did, which he said he would pitch to his team. I didn't tell anyone, because after six years living in Los Angeles, I knew the chances of this actually going anywhere were very slim.

Days went by and then I was contacted by another segment producer. We spoke on the phone, and he asked me to email release forms to all of my parents. Once they'd received the parents' signed release forms, the producers set up a Zoom meeting to go over what Kelly would be asking me during the interview. Well, this was moving quickly. We went over lighting, sound, and then they said there'd be some kind of surprise at the end of the interview. Even Hollywood was having Covid-19 troubles, so the producer said a filming date wasn't set in stone . . . but to be ready. Again, I told very few people, as I assumed a bigger and better story would prevail.

The segment producer called to say the segment would be filmed on a Tuesday afternoon, and Kelly would be taping show segments back to back that day. I scheduled our segment during my lunch. We went over the logistics, and apart from my father and a few close friends, I didn't tell anyone this was happening.

That Tuesday, I transitioned from teaching reading to getting ready for my fifteen minutes of fame. I signed onto the Zoom, waited in the waiting room, and then boom, Kelly appeared on the screen. At first, I wasn't sure if we were just chitchatting behind the scenes, or if the interview had started. But the interview had started, the questions were coming, and I couldn't believe this was all happening! We went to a commercial break, came back to do another segment, and then Kelly said that when we returned from the second break, she would have a surprise for me. It was a few surprise visitors. To my complete and total shock, four of my students and their mothers joined the interview. I was stunned. How was this possible? I had just been teaching them a reading lesson and here they were, on national television with me. How were they able to keep this all a secret?

Kelly asked each student to share something they enjoyed about being in my class and then we played a game. Students asked me questions about things that had happened in our classroom before Covid-19. I won (only getting one question wrong). I then was given an all-inclusive vacation for me and a guest to tropical Punta Mita, Mexico—once travel was safe again. I had never won anything like this before.

Immediately after the interview, I called my dad, my coworker Mary, and my best friend (to tell her I was taking her to Mexico). Right after my appearance on the show, I had an administration meeting where I arrived almost in tears of joy, asking if any of them knew this was happening. They hadn't and were just as surprised as I was. It really was a joyous day. A few days later, my class and I watched the episode when it aired, and I was so happy that a few of them were able to experience this surprise with me.

It wasn't until the summer of 2021 that I began traveling again. I went to Nashville, Tennessee, with my friends Holly and Katie, who were on Teacher Road Trip, where they gave away thousands of dollars in prizes to teachers. Then I spent time with my dad in North Carolina and visited friends and family in New York. My best friend, Jamie, and I took that trip to Mexico, and finally, I spent two days in Atlanta, Georgia, at the Ron Clark Academy celebrating Kim Bearden's fourth book release.

The 2021–2022 school year has been just as challenging as the transition into distance learning. Students haven't had a "normal" school year for three years. I have never worked harder to set up expectations, get students to follow new procedures, collaborate with colleagues, have fun, teach new curriculum, and connect and bond with both students and parents. These normal activities are constantly challenged by weekly Covid-19 testing and the anxiety of waiting to find out if any of my students test positive—which means an immediate pivot back to Zoom. It's all exhausting, and I continue taking it day by day. There's a teaching shortage, and daily I read articles about the mass exodus of teachers from the classroom.

As I mentioned in the preface, the Covid-19 pandemic shone a light on the resource disparity among schools throughout the United States—and even from town to town. After two (plus) years of learning to adapt to living in a Covid-19 world, we are certainly not at the end of a crisis that is crippling the American educational system. I don't know the answer, but I believe it's time for a change. All schools and students should have equal access to technology. It boggles my mind that in 2022, free Wi-Fi doesn't exist in the United States, and there are students with no digital access.

Things We Can Do to Promote Change

1. Vote to get pro-education candidates into offices at all levels of government.
2. Get involved in our school-level decision-making.
3. Support and uplift other educators, including our colleagues. Let's celebrate our successes.
4. Attend professional development to learn new ways to reach our students and execute curriculum.
5. Read professional development books, articles, and stories from other educators. Knowledge is power.
6. Advocate for ourselves and each other. We are only as strong as our weakest link.
7. Avoid interacting with negative coworkers.
8. Leave toxic and/or unsupportive work environments. This is easier said than done, but our mental health and happiness are important.

There are bigger solutions needed, too. America must find a way to keep our best educators in the classroom. Higher teacher salaries, student loan forgiveness, and equitable access to resources must become priorities for our country's leaders. Our government needs to funnel money back into schools to modernize school buildings and provide teachers with updated curricula and professional development. The pandemic has put the focus on educators and the fact that we deserve respect and appreciation from our entire communities.

These have been two exhausting years. As with so many educators, my passion for teaching was almost extinguished. It's time for many of us to recharge our batteries. Writing this book has led me to reflect on the path I've traveled in the last two decades as an educator. And after contemplation, I have decided now is the time for me to move on and reignite my own passion for teaching. I am not leaving the classroom; instead, I am beginning a much-needed new adventure. Recently, I was offered and eagerly accepted an exciting teaching opportunity to start something new. So, just like every other Hollywood blockbuster, you will have to wait for the sequel to find out what happens next.

Let's all reignite our love of teaching—it's the most important job out there, and only you can direct your students toward lifelong success.

Educator Spotlight:
SEL: A Lifeboat, Not a Buzzword

Social emotional learning . . . It's turned into quite the buzzword lately. And to me, it's the BIGGEST word. It's the word that carries the most meaning in my life. It's the word that brings me back to my why. It's the word that continues to push me toward my mission, to be the link that connects all our like-minded, heart-centered educators, district leaders, school administrators, families, and communities, so that we can continue to pour passion into the hearts and minds of our students and children around the world.

Through the pandemic, we've learned that our educators, district leaders, and families are drowning. They're being swallowed up by the mandates, the changes, the shifts, and all the while, more and more things are added to their plates. And not only are the adults struggling, but so are our students and children.

When we give educators a new curriculum, or we ask them to show up and take in the newest or the latest and greatest professional learning, we're giving them a kickboard to use in the current. And at this moment, our teachers don't need a kickboard; they need a lifeboat. They need the tools that will truly transform their classrooms, schools, districts, and homes. They need strategies and systems that will create a common language and transfer from one environment to the next. And they need a framework so that all teachers, classrooms, and schools shift from a focus on behavior toward a focus on supporting our students' lagging social and emotional skills, as well as their academic needs. Being able to work with educators around the world, schools across the country, and families near and far, I've been able to sit back and observe exactly what has been happening in our communities.

It is my mission to be the change agent who continues to give these tools to our educators, schools, and families so that no matter what storm comes our way, or what unknowns are just on  the horizon, we are ready. And we can continue to build our lifeboat so that no one is left drowning ever again.

Kim Gameroz, social-emotional learning consultant, SELebrate Good Times, LLC
@selebrategoodtimes

ACTION!

1. What distance learning tools have you leaned on while teaching during a global pandemic?

2. What lessons have your students learned from being in school during a global pandemic, and where have they suffered learning loss?

3. What changes have you made in your own teaching since 2020?

Acknowledgments

To my parents: I wish my mom could read this book in heaven, and I am glad that my dad will get to hold a copy himself and read it (hopefully displaying it proudly on his living room coffee table). Thank you for all of your support, including supporting my move to La La Land. I would never have made the jump without your encouragement.

To all of my former and future students and their parents: I have learned so much from every single one of you. It's been a joy watching many of you now become adults and pursue your own passions. Thank you for embracing (or putting up with) my out-of-the-box style.

To the Tomasini family: You will always be one of my favorite families. I am grateful that I had both James (twice, ha ha) and Christian as my students and now call all of you my friends. Your support over the years has been ever so appreciated. You were the very first people to visit me in California after my big move, and I always look forward to visiting you when I am in New York.

To some of the administrators I have had over the years: Barbara Lasson, Ken Bossert, Susan Kenny, Sal Alaimo, and Jamilah Ryan. You each helped to mold me into the educator I am today. And for that I will be forever grateful.

To the incredible educators I've been able to call colleagues, several of whom have turned into lifelong friends. Special shout-outs to Jamie Sico, DaNean Cossack, Amy Scala, Elise Allen, Melissa Jordan, Lisa Wells, Gregory Barbera, Nina Smith, Deb Mazura, Michelle Franco, Jacqueline Prokesch, Amanda Vaughn, Tanika Schliebe, Lauren Cantrell, Mary Chen, and Jeannine Brager. You've all been there for good, bad, smooth, and stormy waters.

To those who taught and inspired me to become an educator: Gail Bunce, Nicholas LaGregra, Christine Roelofsen, and Nancy Corso.

To incredible mentors (some of whom never signed up for the position): Ron Clark, Kim Bearden, Dr. Valerie Camile Jones, Adam Dovico, Adam Welcome, Rae Hughart, Alicia Ray, Gerry Brooks, and the MANY other incredible educators I have had the opportunity to learn from.

To the Teach Better team: You motivate, inspire, and uplift educators every day. Thank you for welcoming me to the team.

A special thank-you to Dr. Yvette Ledford for being the very first person to read my manuscript and passionately agreeing to write the foreword to my first book. Your time, energy, and spirit are greatly appreciated.

Eliseo and Dorell: Your friendship came at a time I really needed good people in my life.

Finally, thank you to Dave and Shelley Burgess. Because of you, my childhood dream of being a published author is now true. Thank you for all you do to celebrate the voices of educators.

Resources and References

ALLSIDES

Free

AllSides states that it "strengthens democratic thinking and media literacy with balanced news, diverse perspectives, and real conversation." Its news coverage, media bias ratings, civil dialogue opportunities, and technology platform are available for all and can be integrated by schools.

AMAZON WISH LIST

Free

Teachers (or anyone) can create wish lists with items they need. An Amazon wish list can be shared and fulfilled by anyone who has the link. I share my classroom wish list with parents at Back to School Night each year.

BLOOKET

Free with a paid option

Blooket describes itself as a "new take on trivia and review games." A teacher or host selects any subject area and game mode. The game modes come in a variety of gaming styles and look very similar to a video game. Then, Blooket generates a code that players use to join the game on their own devices. After the game starts, players answer content questions to help them win. Blooket can be used after a mini-lesson, for independent practice, or at the end of a longer unit of study.

DONORSCHOOSE
Free

DonorsChoose supports public school teachers in getting materials they need for their students. Teachers upload a project for which they need funding, donors fund projects, and teachers are sent the materials they requested. Then, teachers and students send donors a thank-you.

EPIC!
Free and paid

Epic! is a digital reading platform with a huge collection of popular, high-quality books from various publishers, designed to foster a love of reading for kids ages twelve and under.

FLOCABULARY
One month free, then a paid monthly subscription

Flocabulary offers catchy, memorable hip-hop-style songs for a variety of subject areas. In addition to songs, the Flocabulary site includes lesson resources, standard alignments, and review activities. Suitable for all grades and subjects.

FLIPGRID
Free

Flipgrid's free video discussion app provides a safe, accessible space for students of all ages, abilities, and backgrounds to explore new ideas, connect with others, and get creative. Flipgrid Live offers educators the opportunity for their students to meet and interact with some of the world's most fascinating people, such as Stacey Abrams,

Chelsea Clinton, Mike Smith, Ruth Kapp Hartz, Peter Reynolds, and many more.

GILDER LEHRMAN INSTITUTE OF AMERICAN HISTORY
Free

The Gilder Lehrman Institute of American History is a nonprofit organization dedicated to K–12 history education. Its goal is to promote an understanding of American history through educational programs and resources.

ICIVICS
Free

iCivics is the nation's premier nonprofit civic education provider of free, engaging, high-quality, nonpartisan resources. iCivics' digital civic library includes more than 260 curricular resources, digital literacy tools, professional learning materials, and educational video games. Their engaging resources help to improve civic knowledge and skills.

KIDS DISCOVER MAGAZINES
Paid, with some free resources

Kids Discover magazines focus on social studies and science topics. Their team is "committed to a single mission: to get children excited about reading and learning with their library of nonfiction material." Their materials are available both in print and online.

MOOD METER
Free

Yale's Center for Emotional Learning describes the Mood Meter as "one of the 'anchors of Emotional Intelligence' in the RULER program. It helps people develop the core RULER skills: Recognizing,

Understanding, Labeling, Expressing, and Regulating emotions. The Mood Meter develops emotional intelligence over time. Learning to identify and label emotions is a critical step toward cultivating emotional intelligence. Using the Mood Meter can help you become more mindful of how your emotions change throughout the day and how your emotions in turn affect your actions."

NEWSELA
Free and paid options

"Newsela is a literacy-focused edtech startup company offering grade-leveled and standards-aligned informational content in English and Spanish." The topics throughout the site include current events, social studies, SEL, and science. Additional features and resources are available for English language learners.

QUIZIZZ
Free or paid

Quizizz is a gamified student engagement platform that offers multiple features to make classroom lessons fun, interactive, and engaging. Teachers can conduct formative assessments, assign homework, and create review activities for any grade and subject. Games can be teacher- or student-paced.

STUDIES WEEKLY
Paid subscription

Studies Weekly is a periodical supplement for K–6 students that can be used as a standards-based core curriculum for social studies, science, and SEL. Each week, a new issue containing fresh content is published, and the teacher edition contains resources and activities to engage students in learning.

REMIND

Free

This is a safe, easy tool for either one-way or two-way communication between teachers and students and their families. The Remind app is available in the Apple or Google Play Store.

WONDEROPOLIS

Free

Wonderopolis is a website that helps students learn about almost any subject. Each day, Wonderoplis poses a new question and explores it in a variety of ways. Wonderopolis was created in 2010 by the National Center for Families Learning (NCFL), and it has quickly become one of the most popular edtech sites used in classrooms.

About the Author

In 2002, Kevin Butler began teaching in New York at a suburban public school on Long Island, New York. In 2014, he relocated to California to work at a start-up charter school in the city of Los Angeles. Most recently, Kevin has taught fifth grade and was also the coordinator for curriculum and instruction at an independent school in the suburbs of Los Angeles. His instruction focuses on creating authentic relationships with his students while engaging them in rigorous, hands-on learning.

Kevin has been a guest on several educational podcasts and blogs, where he has shared ideas on engaging students in active learning and the importance of building and maintaining classroom relationships. In the spring of 2020, Kevin was a guest on *The Kelly Clarkson Show*, where he discussed pathways to creating student connections during the Covid-19 crisis. Later in 2020, Kevin was featured in the book *Teachers Deserve It* by Adam Welcome and Rae Hughart. Kevin has also appeared in the *Hollywood Reporter*, where he shared how his Morning Co-Host Show teaches students communication skills and helps build classroom culture.

In addition to teaching, Kevin speaks and presents at national educator conferences throughout the United States, including Teach Better, ASCD, and Teach Your Heart Out. Kevin also enjoys visiting schools and facilitating sessions and workshops on student engagement, classroom culture, and the importance of building relationships with students, parents, and colleagues. In his free time, Kevin enjoys traveling, hiking, relaxing at the beach, and being out in nature. You can often find Kevin working out at Barry's Bootcamp, sipping coffee at a local coffee shop, or buying a new houseplant at a local garden shop.

This fall, Kevin is extremely excited to be kicking off his twentieth year as a classroom teacher. Kevin can be found on social media at @thekevinjbutler and at thekevinjbutler.com.

More from

Dave Burgess Consulting, Inc.

Since 2012, DBCI has published books that inspire and equip educators to be their best. For more information on our titles or to purchase bulk orders for your school, district, or book study, visit DaveBurgessConsulting.com/DBCIbooks.

THE *LIKE A PIRATE*™ SERIES
Teach Like a PIRATE by Dave Burgess
eXPlore Like a PIRATE by Michael Matera
Learn Like a PIRATE by Paul Solarz
Plan Like a PIRATE by Dawn M. Harris
Play Like a PIRATE by Quinn Rollins
Run Like a PIRATE by Adam Welcome
Tech Like a PIRATE by Matt Miller

LEAD *LIKE A PIRATE*™ SERIES
Lead Like a PIRATE by Shelley Burgess and Beth Houf
Balance Like a PIRATE by Jessica Cabeen, Jessica Johnson, and
 Sarah Johnson
Lead beyond Your Title by Nili Bartley
Lead with Appreciation by Amber Teamann and Melinda Miller
Lead with Culture by Jay Billy
Lead with Instructional Rounds by Vicki Wilson
Lead with Literacy by Mandy Ellis
She Leads by Dr. Rachael George and Majalise W. Tolan

LEADERSHIP & SCHOOL CULTURE
Beyond the Surface of Restorative Practices by Marisol Rerucha
Change the Narrative by Henry J. Turner and Kathy Lopes
Choosing to See by Pamela Seda and Kyndall Brown
Culturize by Jimmy Casas
Discipline Win by Andy Jacks

Escaping the School Leader's Dunk Tank by Rebecca Coda and
    Rick Jetter
Fight Song by Kim Bearden
From Teacher to Leader by Starr Sackstein
If the Dance Floor Is Empty, Change the Song by Joe Clark
The Innovator's Mindset by George Couros
It's OK to Say "They" by Christy Whittlesey
Kids Deserve It! by Todd Nesloney and Adam Welcome
Let Them Speak by Rebecca Coda and Rick Jetter
The Limitless School by Abe Hege and Adam Dovico
Live Your Excellence by Jimmy Casas
Next-Level Teaching by Jonathan Alsheimer
The Pepper Effect by Sean Gaillard
Principaled by Kate Barker, Kourtney Ferrua, and Rachael George
The Principled Principal by Jeffrey Zoul and Anthony McConnell
Relentless by Hamish Brewer
The Secret Solution by Todd Whitaker, Sam Miller, and Ryan Donlan
Start. Right. Now. by Todd Whitaker, Jeffrey Zoul, and Jimmy Casas
Stop. Right. Now. by Jimmy Casas and Jeffrey Zoul
Teachers Deserve It by Rae Hughart and Adam Welcome
Teach Your Class Off by CJ Reynolds
They Call Me "Mr. De" by Frank DeAngelis
Thrive through the Five by Jill M. Siler
Unmapped Potential by Julie Hasson and Missy Lennard
When Kids Lead by Todd Nesloney and Adam Dovico
Word Shift by Joy Kirr
Your School Rocks by Ryan McLane and Eric Lowe

TECHNOLOGY & TOOLS
50 Things to Go Further with Google Classroom by Alice Keeler and
    Libbi Miller
50 Things You Can Do with Google Classroom by Alice Keeler and
    Libbi Miller
140 Twitter Tips for Educators by Brad Currie, Billy Krakower, and
    Scott Rocco
Block Breaker by Brian Aspinall
Building Blocks for Tiny Techies by Jamila "Mia" Leonard

Code Breaker by Brian Aspinall

The Complete EdTech Coach by Katherine Goyette and Adam Juarez

Control Alt Achieve by Eric Curts

The Esports Education Playbook by Chris Aviles, Steve Isaacs, Christine Lion-Bailey, and Jesse Lubinsky

Google Apps for Littles by Christine Pinto and Alice Keeler

Master the Media by Julie Smith

Raising Digital Leaders by Jennifer Casa-Todd

Reality Bytes by Christine Lion-Bailey, Jesse Lubinsky, and Micah Shippee, PhD

Sail the 7 Cs with Microsoft Education by Becky Keene and Kathi Kersznowski

Shake Up Learning by Kasey Bell

Social LEADia by Jennifer Casa-Todd

Stepping Up to Google Classroom by Alice Keeler and Kimberly Mattina

Teaching Math with Google Apps by Alice Keeler and Diana Herrington

Teachingland by Amanda Fox and Mary Ellen Weeks

Teaching with Google Jamboard by Alice Keeler and Kimberly Mattina

TEACHING METHODS & MATERIALS

All 4s and 5s by Andrew Sharos

Boredom Busters by Katie Powell

The Classroom Chef by John Stevens and Matt Vaudrey

The Collaborative Classroom by Trevor Muir

Copyrighteous by Diana Gill

CREATE by Bethany J. Petty

Deploying EduProtocols by Kim Voge, with Jon Corippo and Marlena Hebern

Ditch That Homework by Matt Miller and Alice Keeler

Ditch That Textbook by Matt Miller

Don't Ditch That Tech by Matt Miller, Nate Ridgway, and Angelia Ridgway

EDrenaline Rush by John Meehan

Educated by Design by Michael Cohen, The Tech Rabbi

The EduProtocol Field Guide by Marlena Hebern and Jon Corippo

The EduProtocol Field Guide: Book 2 by Marlena Hebern and Jon Corippo

The EduProtocol Field Guide: Math Edition by Lisa Nowakowski and
     Jeremiah Ruesch
Expedition Science by Becky Schnekser
Frustration Busters by Katie Powell
Fully Engaged by Michael Matera and John Meehan
Game On? Brain On! by Lindsay Portnoy, PhD
Guided Math AMPED by Reagan Tunstall
Innovating Play by Jessica LaBar-Twomy and Christine Pinto
Instructional Coaching Connection by Nathan Lang-Raad
Instant Relevance by Denis Sheeran
Keeping the Wonder by Jenna Copper, Ashley Bible, Abby Gross, and
     Staci Lamb
LAUNCH by John Spencer and A.J. Juliani
Make Learning MAGICAL by Tisha Richmond
Pass the Baton by Kathryn Finch and Theresa Hoover
Project-Based Learning Anywhere by Lori Elliott
Pure Genius by Don Wettrick
The Revolution by Darren Ellwein and Derek McCoy
Shift This! by Joy Kirr
Skyrocket Your Teacher Coaching by Michael Cary Sonbert
Spark Learning by Ramsey Musallam
Sparks in the Dark by Travis Crowder and Todd Nesloney
Table Talk Math by John Stevens
Unpack Your Impact by Naomi O'Brien and LaNesha Tabb
The Wild Card by Hope and Wade King
Writefully Empowered by Jacob Chastain
The Writing on the Classroom Wall by Steve Wyborney
You Are Poetry by Mike Johnston

INSPIRATION, PROFESSIONAL GROWTH & PERSONAL DEVELOPMENT

Be REAL by Tara Martin
Be the One for Kids by Ryan Sheehy
The Coach ADVenture by Amy Illingworth
Creatively Productive by Lisa Johnson
Educational Eye Exam by Alicia Ray

The EduNinja Mindset by Jennifer Burdis

Empower Our Girls by Lynmara Colón and Adam Welcome

Finding Lifelines by Andrew Grieve and Andrew Sharos

The Four O'Clock Faculty by Rich Czyz

How Much Water Do We Have? by Pete and Kris Nunweiler

P Is for Pirate by Dave and Shelley Burgess

A Passion for Kindness by Tamara Letter

The Path to Serendipity by Allyson Apsey

Rogue Leader by Rich Czyz

Sanctuaries by Dan Tricarico

Saving Sycamore by Molly B. Hudgens

The SECRET SAUCE by Rich Czyz

Shattering the Perfect Teacher Myth by Aaron Hogan

Stories from Webb by Todd Nesloney

Talk to Me by Kim Bearden

Teach Better by Chad Ostrowski, Tiffany Ott, Rae Hughart, and Jeff Gargas

Teach Me, Teacher by Jacob Chastain

Teach, Play, Learn! by Adam Peterson

The Teachers of Oz by Herbie Raad and Nathan Lang-Raad

TeamMakers by Laura Robb and Evan Robb

Through the Lens of Serendipity by Allyson Apsey

The Zen Teacher by Dan Tricarico

CHILDREN'S BOOKS

Beyond Us by Aaron Polansky

Cannonball In by Tara Martin

Dolphins in Trees by Aaron Polansky

I Can Achieve Anything by MoNique Waters

I Want to Be a Lot by Ashley Savage

Micah's Big Question by Naomi O'Brien

The Princes of Serendip by Allyson Apsey

Ride with Emilio by Richard Nares

The Wild Card Kids by Hope and Wade King

Zom-Be a Design Thinker by Amanda Fox

Made in the USA
Las Vegas, NV
11 August 2022

53097986R10127